Senegal Behind Glass

Images of Religious and Daily Life

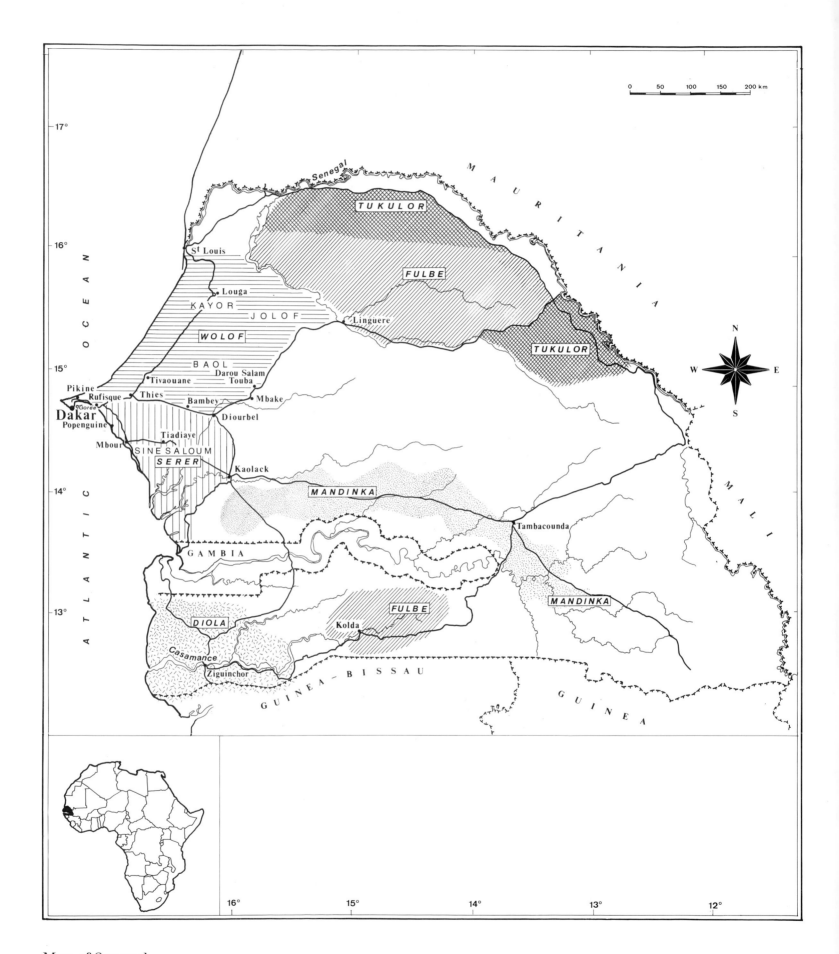

Map of Senegal

Anne-Marie Bouttiaux-Ndiaye

Senegal
Behind Glass

Images of Religious and Daily Life

Prestel

Munich · New York

This book was published on the occasion of the travelling exhibition
'Hinterglasmalerei aus dem Senegal' organized by

The Royal Museum of Central Africa, Tervuren

and first held at the Hamburgisches Museum für Völkerkunde, Hamburg
(30 June–18 September 1994), and continuing on to further venues.

© 1994 by Prestel-Verlag, Munich and New York, and the Royal Museum
of Central Africa, Tervuren
© of all texts by Anne-Marie Bouttiaux-Ndiaye
© of illustrated works by the artists
Photographic acknowledgements, see p. 167

Front cover: Babacar Lo, *Portrait of a Woman*, 1993 (plate 123)
Back cover: Azu Bade, *Cooking*, 1994 (plate 86)
Frontispiece: map of Senegal by Jacqueline Renard

Prestel-Verlag
Mandlstrasse 26, 80802 Munich, Germany, Tel. (89) 3817090; Fax (89) 38170935
and 16 West 22nd Street, New York, NY 10010, USA, Tel. (212) 6278199;
Fax (212) 6279866

Distributed in other countries on behalf of Prestel as follows:

Australia: by PERIBO PTY Limited, 26 Tepko Road, Terrey Hills NSW 2084

Austria: by Heidrich & Lechner, Postfach 105, 1232 Wien-Blumenthal

France: by INTERART S.A.R.L. 108, rue de Couronnes, 75020

Japan: by YOHAN Western Publications Distribution Agency, 14–9 Okubo 3-chome,
Shijuku-ku, Tokyo 169

Netherlands and Belgium: by Nilsson and Lamm, Pampuslaan 212, 1380 AD Weesp

Switzerland: by Dr. A. Scheidegger, Obere Bahnhofstrasse 10A, 8910 Affoltern am Albis

United Kingdom, Ireland, the Commonwealth (except Australia), and all countries
except continental Europe, USA, Canada and Japan: by Thames & Hudson Limited,
30–34 Bloomsbury Street, London WC1B 3QP

USA and Canada: by te Neues Publishing Company, 16 West 22nd Street, New York,
NY 10010, USA

Translated from the French by Martine Jawerbaum with Jill Craig
Copy-edited by Robert Williams

Designed by Heinz Ross, Munich
Cover design by Fritz Lüdtke and Adam Volohonsky, Munich
Typeset by Passavia GmbH, Passau
Offset lithography by Lithovertrieb Horst H. Bruch, Germering
Printed and bound by Friedrich Pustet GmbH & Co. KG, Regensburg

Printed in Germany

ISBN 3-7913-1424-6 (hardcover edition)

Acknowledgements

We wish to thank all those who have generously lent works from their collections for inclusion in the exhibition and which are reproduced in this book: ADA (Africa, Diaspora and Art), Brussels; M. and Mme Cherot, Lille; Mme Marie-Laure Croiziers de Lacvivier, Paris; Maurice Dedieu, Paris; M. and Mme Doneux, Brussels; Yvon Dupré for the Soleils des Francophonies Association, Brech; Jean-Pierre Jacquemin, Brussels; Kelountang Ndiaye, Brussels; Bernard Schoeffer, Paris; M. and Mme Renaudeau, Paris; Dirk Thys van den Audenaerde, Wezembeek-Oppem; and also the Royal Museum of Central Africa, Tervuren, and the Royal Museums of Art and History, Brussels.

We would like to pay a special tribute to all those Senegalese artists included in this book, without whose assistance our project could never have been realized: Azu Bade, Fode Camara, Sea Diallo, Arona Diarra, Gabou, Mor Gueye, Moussa Johnson, Jules, Khaly, Souleymane Keita, Babacar Lo, Moussa Lo, Mallos, Mbida, Metzo, Cheikh Ndao, Magatte Ndiaye, Serigne Ndiaye, Alexis Ngom, Paco, Ibrahima Sall, Hassane Sar, and Amadou Sow. Among this list of painters is one who does not work in the genre of reverse-glass, yet it is to him that we owe the greatest debt – Fode Camara, who accompanied us everywhere, introduced us to numerous artists and who encouraged us every day. For his enthusiasm, his generosity and his unfailing help, we dedicate this book to him.

Dr Dirk Thys van den Audenaerde, Director of the Royal Museum of Central Africa, Tervuren, and Dr Gustaaf Verswijver, Curator of the Museum's Ethnography Section, were unstinting in their efforts to ensure that things ran smoothly for us at every stage of organizing the exhibition and writing this book.

Our thanks, also, to Kelountang Ndiaye for his sound advice; to Jean Doneux for his guidance regarding Wolof transcriptions; and to Sabine Cornelis, Sophie Decock, Els De Palmenaer, Wilfried Ficrmans, Martine Jawerbaum, Kaleunkwe Ndiaye, Mandionka Ndiaye, Nalla Ndiaye, Jacqueline Renard, Jean Marc Vandyck, Vredeseilanden, and Catherine Weynants.

Foreword

Modern art in Africa is a controversial subject. Unlike traditional art, it is young, still evolving, and its origins are often unclear. The roots of traditional African art, on the other hand, were, and remain, firmly secured in the social and cultural life of the people, although, strictly speaking, there is no such thing as traditional African *art*. Ritual objects, for example masks, statues of ancestors, sceptres and other regalia, were always made in accordance with local tradition; their size, shape and style were not individually determined by the personal whims of their makers, but always conformed to the traditional, functional requirements of the tribe.

For many centuries Westerners considered African objects to be little more than exotic curiosities. Not until the beginning of our own century did some Western artists, for example Maurice de Vlaminck, André Derain and Picasso, discover the unusual, indeed pronounced, aesthetic aspects of African objects. From that time forward, such objects have exerted a strong influence on many Western artists, and by degrees they have been assimilated into the world of fine-art production.

Under the impact of Western colonization, which corroded established patterns of African rural life and induced the formation of those urban environments that today continue to replace them, traditional (handcrafted) modes of production declined drastically. In the towns, African craftsmen switched to mass-producing degraded copies of traditional crafts for Western consumption. In some parts of Africa colonial governments attempted to halt this trend: Western-style art schools were opened where Africans were taught drawing, painting, textile-weaving and sculpture (mostly wood). Debate continues as to whether the new works should be seen as making an authentic contribution to twentieth-century art or as largely derivative. Clearly, all these trends and art forms have one thing in common: they were initiated under the influence of European teaching, their techniques derived from the same source, and their market was wholly a Western one.

The *Souweres*, or reverse-glass paintings, of Senegal are a notable exception to this trend, however. Having begun as a local craft that afterwards developed into a popular art, reverse-glass painting remains the only type of graphic art in Africa that developed entirely without influence from white colonists.

Today, reverse-glass paintings provide an income for a number of artists living in urban areas. Since the beginning of the nineteenth century when works were anonymous, much of the original inspiration and subject-matter has disappeared and in the 1990s the business is rife with the ill-trained copyists who compete with talented artists in what is still a limited market. But although it can no longer be claimed that current reverse-glass painting is a genuine 'African' art – that is, by Africans for

Africans–some of its practitioners continue to preserve aspects of a century-old traditional, yet also *modern*, art in Senegal.

The Tervuren Museum, and its Department of Cultural Anthropology, have been dedicated since their foundation almost exclusively to Africa's ethnographic art and to the study and collection of its artefacts. Recently, art of more modern times has received some attention, but traditional works continue to be the Museum's chief focus of interest. For over a decade the Museum has been actively involved in collecting and researching Senegalese reverse-glass painting, from the earliest examples to the most recent, and has cooperated enthusiastically with Anne-Marie Bouttiaux-Ndiaye in order to add to the collection and to make possible this present exhibition. The Museum is proud to be able to present this survey of Senegalese reverse-glass painting, and sees it as a salute to the many anonymous artists who, over the decades, have contributed to it. Through their efforts, a vivid, colourful pictorial tradition has been sustained (as has a good deal of popular wisdom) without it having received any real financial support. Their contribution to modern African art–and to art more generally–should not be forgotten.

Dr D. Thys van den Audenaerde
Director,
Royal Museum of Central Africa

Senegalese reverse-glass painting

1 Among the recent exhibitions largely devoted to Senegalese reverse-glass painting are the following. Senegal: '50 fixés sous-verre sénégalais', Atelier Renaudeau, June 1977; 'Peinture sous verre du Sénégal', Gallery of the Centre d'Echange culturel de la langue française, 27 November-22 December 1984. USA: 'Senegal Narrative Paintings' (the Maurice Dedieu collection), University Art Museum, Lafayette, Louisiana, 12 January-15 February 1985; 'Treasures of a Popular Art: Paintings on Glass from Senegal', African-American Institute, New York, 27 March-26 September 1986. France: 'Peintures populaires du Senegal – Souweres', National Museum of African and Oceanian Arts, Paris, May-September 1987. Belgium: 'Un œil de verre – Souweres et vitrines', La Papeterie, Brussels, 18-28 January 1990; 'Peintures sous verre du Senegal', Royal Museum of Central Africa, Tervuren, 24 November 1993-30 January 1994.

The art of reverse-glass painting was at its domestic peak in Senegal earlier this century, between the 1920s and the 1960s. At that time it was produced by Senegalese for Senegalese, but the situation began to change once it had caught the attention of European collectors; today, it is chiefly produced for Western tourists and collectors. It remains unclear whether few Senegalese buy this kind of art nowadays simply because it is unfashionable, or because prices rocketed once Western visitors had become interested in acquiring examples. Perhaps it is a combination of the two that has resulted in the disappearance of works of this kind from African homes. Even so, few recent exhibitions of African art held in Europe or North America have failed to include examples;[1] attention is drawn to its aesthetic and commercial value, and also to its didactic nature, for however naive, colourful and funny these pictures might at first appear, they are cultural testimonies of primary significance: some recall nostalgically the glorious deeds and simple life of past times, others present ideological and religious propaganda. Reverse-glass painting is an art-form that is still too often relegated to the rank of 'minor art', with all the contempt this entails. Even if recent production has, under the influence of tourism, revealed a regrettable drop in quality, artists of great value still remain to defend this form of expression: holders of the tradition from the old generation, for example Gora Mbengue (see p. 24), or those rising artists that combine a respect for tradition with novel developments. This is the reason why, in addition to the usual historic and thematic presentations, this book also presents the various personalities who create reverse-glass paintings. The artists themselves want their art to be reconsidered in this way now that the practice of signing their works has been established. Some of them, like Babacar Lo (pp. 25-6), find examples of their earlier, unsigned pieces at exhibitions and remain perplexed at the prices that of these 'anonymous' paintings reach in the West! Others, like Mbida (pp. 27-8), who is very popular among European collectors and whose works sell at particularly high prices, have become real celebrities. But this success often brings drawbacks with it, and the most sought after and expensive artists are also those who are the most mercilessly exploited and plagiarized.

Terminology and technique

Following German and Dutch precedent, where paintings made on the back of glass are called *Hinterglasmalerei* and *achterglasschilderij* respectively, we have coined the term 'reverse-glass painting'. To speak of 'behind-glass' painting generates ambiguity, and it hardly conveys an

Fig. 1 Babacar Lo drawing the outlines in indian ink, July 1993.

idea of the basic technique, which involves work *performed on the back* of a sheet of glass. (Although 'back-of-glass' removes all ambiguities, it is dreadfully cumbersome.) The term *églomisé*,[2] widely used by historians of the decorative arts, refers specifically to a technique that involves decorating glass by means of gilding, while the expression 'fixed under glass' refers, of course, to pictures pasted behind or framed under glass.[3] The word 'fixed' is, none the less, frequently encountered in the literature on Senegalese art, and, if its application is often incorrect, it is sometimes partially appropriate in a few early examples where both techniques – painting and pasting – are combined: these examples are

Fig. 2 The stages in painting a reverse-glass work: *Woman with a Parrot*, now in the Royal Museum of Central Africa, Tervuren. The drawing on paper that is used as the design to trace behind the glass.

Fig. 3 Reverse-glass drawing in indian ink after the design on paper illustrated in fig. 2.

Fig. 4 The first colour details applied in the spaces defined by the indian ink outlines.

Figs. 5/6 More colour is added. Some of the garment motifs are created directly at this stage. In the center is the front of the work, to the right the reverse, revealing the superimposition of layers of paint: note that the first details have disappeared under fresh colour. The artist, in error, has signed the work – and the wrong way around – as if it were a finished painting!

2 In the *Larousse Universel* French dictionary, the adjective 'eglomisé' is defined as the description of an object made in glass that is 'decorated by means of an inner gilding', although 'verre églomisé' is widely used to mean 'glass that is decorated on the back by unfired painting or, usually, by gilding' (John Fleming and Hugh Honour, *The Penguin Dictionary of Decorative Arts*, London, 1979, p. 826). The term was coined by Jean-Baptist Glomy, an eighteenth-century Parisian picture-framer who decorated glass picture-mounts by means of engraved gold leaves.

3 Bourlard, pp. 132-4.

4 The Wolof are the largest of Senegal's ethnic groups, and their language the one most widely spoken. Currently, the largest number of reverse-glass painters are to be found among the Wolof, although increasingly members of other ethnic groups are learning the technique.

5 Dancu, p. 10.

chromolithographs (plate 1) or photographs (plates 2-4) that have been placed behind painted glass. Finally, in Senegal, glass paintings are called *suwer*, a Wolof[4] word directly borrowed from the French *sous-verre* (behind or under glass). By extension, *suwer* is the term that is also used to emphasize the qualities of culinary dishes made with a great variety of ingredients: a *ceebu jën* (rice with fish) is called *ceeb suwer* when it is richly decorated and colourful.

The first step in making a reverse-glass painting consists of drawing the outlines in indian ink on the back of the glass. To achieve this, the artist can draw freehand directly on the glass (fig. 1) or trace a pattern (figs. 2 and 3). It is at this initial stage that he must add his signature or any inscriptions required, executing them backwards (from right to left or, for Arabic characters, from left to right) so that they will be visible from the front. The colours come next, filling the spaces created by the outlines, starting with the details (figs. 4-6). The background, which is the last to be applied, sometimes covers the whole of the picture (fig. 7). The process is thus the reverse of that used when creating a work on canvas or on paper, where the background is the first coat of colour that is applied. In the reverse-glass process, the glass is both the medium for and the protection of the painting,[5] making it transparent, luminous, insubstantial and fragile. But note that at any one stage of creating a reverse-glass painting, the artist has little or no opportunity to correct or revise. At the very most he can, during the initial stages, rework ink outlines or remove smears of colour by scraping with a razor-blade. Superimposing coats of paint from the initial details towards the overall pictorial effect makes it impossible to modify the first lines at a later stage, which are also the most important in that they are the features of a work that the spectator perceives first.

Origins and evolution

Glass appears to have originated around 1500 BC in western Asia (present-day Syria and Iraq).[6] Not until Roman times do we find the first examples of dishes or objects that have been decorated with gold leaf at the back of the glass, and by the 2nd century AD there were cases of

Fig.8 *Virgin with Coat*, 19th century, 47×37 cm (18.5×14.5 in), Royal Museums of Art and History, Brussels. Like so many Senegalese works, this anonymous Polish painting is charged with piety and devotion: the image, too, goes beyond realism, as the disproportionate size of the Virgin indicates.

paintings that were truly executed behind glass, thus intended to be viewed from the other side, an early form of transparency. Most surviving examples are bowls, in which the base presents a picture by means of three or four superimposed colours.[7] This Roman tradition of painted glass spread across the Mediterranean world, as far east as Byzantium.[8] By the Middle Ages in Italy, and in central and in western Europe, engraved gold leaf was being applied on broad glass plates, that is to say on an extensive, flat surface, and no longer on dishes or medallions. The first real reverse-glass paintings were produced during the Renaissance; these tended to be copies of works by the great masters of the time, and were thus a relatively 'scholarly' art. As far as popular art goes, it was in central and eastern Europe that reverse-glass paintings enjoyed their period of glory in the eighteenth and nineteenth centuries.[9] The invention of chromolithography (colour printing using the lithograph technique) in the 1830s contributed to their disappearance from the European scene,[10] by which time, however, interest in reverse-glass painting was spreading throughout the world to the Middle East, China, India, the Americas, and, of course, Black Africa, particularly Senegal. If one compares popular examples from Europe and from Senegal, one notes many common features: outlines, flat washes of colour, religious themes, hieratic, static figures, and deliberate disproportions and freedom from Renaissance laws of perspective, these not out of clumsiness but for emphasis (fig. 8).

History of the Senegalese technique

Reverse-glass painting in Senegal originated in the late nineteenth century. Although the technique seems to have spread from Maghreb, especially Tunisia, which was then under the influence of both Italy and Turkey, one should not discard the possibility that it may have reached Senegal from the Near East, introduced by Moslem pilgrims returning from Mecca.[11] Either way, its introduction to Black Africa is connected with Islam, a religion that was followed in Senegal in the tenth century[12] and established in the one following.[13] Two important interventions contributed to the development of reverse-glass paintings: the introduction by Moroccan and Lebano-Syrian merchants of Moslem votive pictures in the form of chromolithographs (plate 1), mechanically printed in large numbers, and their suppression by the French colonial administration. William Ponty,[14] then Governor of French West Africa, feared the perverse effects of these images, and by perverse effects one means conversion, en masse, to Islam. In November 1911 he sent a standard letter to the various lieutenant-governors forbidding circulation of chromolithographs. Aware that he was in contravention of the law of 29 July 1881 on the freedom of the press in Senegal, Ponty feared provoking the hostility of the population. For this reason he insisted on distinguishing between purely religious publications (the Koran, prayer-books, etc.) and those books, papers, brochures and images that had something of a seditious character. He specifically mentioned the Syrian and Moroccan mer-

6 Harden, p. 3.
7 Painter, pp. 259-61.
8 Boisdur, p. 223.
9 Bourlard, pp. 136-42.
10 'Souweres', p. 11.
11 Boisdur, p. 227.
12 Sy, p. 414.
13 Samb, 1971, p. 463.
14 William Ponty (1866-1915) was the Governor of French West Africa from 1908 to 1915; for an account of his administration see Johnson, *passim*.

chants who had arrived in the colony carrying 'abnormal quantities of publications of all kinds written in Arabic' along with 'rough colour engravings representing scenes from Moslem religious life'. He argued that such prints encouraged interest in the religion of the Prophet and promoted Islam's expansion, and decided that all publications displaying a 'hostile character' towards the civilizing work of the colonial administration, or those 'simply likely to favour maraboutic action' should be destroyed.[15] It was in reaction to this interdiction that the Senegalese harnessed the technique of reverse-glass painting to copy the few religious prints they already possessed.[16] This explains why it is that the earliest works in the medium are mostly traditional images of the Moslem religion, and that they were to be found only in places such as Dakar, Rufisque, St-Louis and Kaolack, for these were the cities the Lebano-Syrian merchants visited, bringing with them the necessary materials – first the glass, then later indian inks, brushes and manufactured paints. Unlike the situation in Europe and the Middle East at that time, where images produced mechanically or photographically superseded ones made by local artists, in Senegal, paradoxically, it is these very techniques that encouraged the development of reverse-glass painting: chromolithography because its prints were illegal and because there was a strong demand for the subject-matter illustrated in them, and photography because it was then still a very expensive process.[17] And yet, photography has always enjoyed a privileged relationship with reverse-glass paintings, for the earliest painters often worked on the reverse side of the protective glass of old photographs, adding animal or floral backgrounds in order to enhance the photographed image (plates 2, 3, 4); later, they themselves translated onto the glass the poses people strike when in front of a camera (plate 127). Moreover, their source of inspiration was often a photograph; and if sometimes it was a reference drawing, rarely was it a living model (plate 134).

Reverse-glass painting thus appeared as the least costly way of getting around the interdiction on reproductions of Moslem votive images. Indeed, less than thirty years ago it was still possible to find a reverse-glass painting for the price of CFA 50, i.e. less than US $ 0.20![18]

Themes

Islam and Senegalese brotherhoods

For the most part, the earliest reverse-glass paintings derive their subject-matter from traditional Islamic themes. These were drawn from the Koran (and from the Bible, whose Book of Genesis the Koran follows[19]) and revived the iconography of the first Islamic images circulated in Senegal in the late nineteenth century and early in the twentieth.[20] The interdiction on figurative art that related to Islam was certainly of no concern to Senegalese artists of the time, not least because the Koran makes no pronouncements about what is deemed improper in art. Moreover, early Moslem conquests had included regions of great artistic ex-

15 In a letter addressed to the Minister for the Colonies, Ponty observed that 'nobody could deny what a wonderful tool of propaganda is created here by the circulation, among people that are not only ignorant but – it is important not to forget – naive, impressionable and still impregnated with old fetishistic superstitions via thousands of copies of these rough, very colourful, engravings, which present the defenders of the sole religion in the most favourable light, addressing, in a word, imagination rather than intelligence, and accompanied moreover by comments appropriate to the needs of the cause'. Cynically, Ponty also pointed out that the money spent on these pictures was lost to the tax collector and to local business. Later he was even to suggest that the Ministry circulate chromolithographs portraying illustrious Frenchmen or glorious deeds from French history (National Archives of Senegal, file 19 G 4). But despite his intolerant, imperialist stance, Ponty does appear to have been able to assess the meaning contained in these pictures more acutely than most of our contemporaries, who see nothing in them but naive and meaningless figures.

16 Strobel, p. 13.

17 Vogel, pp. 117, 119.

18 In fact, less than US$ 0.10, if one takes the devaluation of 11 January 1994 into account!

19 Gaudefroy-Demombynes, p. 286.

20 Strobel, p. 13.

21 Aziza, pp. 42-54.

22 Shiitism is the doctrine that recognizes Ali as the sole successor of Mohammed and rejects his other descendants – Abu Bakr, Othman and Omar – who are recognized by those Moslems who subscribe to Sunnite orthodoxy.

23 Strobel, p. 24.

24 Samb, 1971, p. 469.

25 Strobel, p. 24.

26 Sufism is the doctrine of Islamic mystics who practice asceticism in order to reach a supreme state of grace, one in fusion with Allah, or God. In the ninth century AD this movement appeared in the Middle East, where the first mystics became popular saints. It spread to North Africa around the twelfth century and became associated with those brotherhoods that promoted the cult of worshipping saints. Sufism reached Senegal in the late eighteenth century and early nineteenth (Cruise O'Brien, pp. 26-7).

27 Monteil, 1964, pp. 122-3, 139; Moreau, p. 191.

Fig. 9 Babacar Lo, *Adam and Eve*, 1994, 48 × 33 cm (19 × 13 in), Royal Museum of Central Africa, Tervuren.

cellence and long tradition, such as Byzantium and Persia, and the iconoclastic trend had already suffered many reversals.[21] For this reason, the earliest Senegalese reverse-glass paintings, including calligraphy (plate 5), architecture (plate 6) and animals, would certainly not be considered anterior to those showing human beings: the slow progression towards human imagery in Islamic art took place long before Islamic-inspired art had gained a foothold in Senegal.

Traditional themes recall great moments in the history of humanity, such as those that are presented in the Bible – Adam and Eve, Noah's Ark (figs. 9, 10) Abraham's sacrifice (plate 8), the Nativity (plate 7) – or illustrate various episodes in the life of Mohammed, his successors, and the saints of Moslem history: the ascension of the Prophet riding Al Boraq, the Agony of the Damned, the Hegira, the Battle of Badr, the Four Caliphs and Bilal, the scenes relating to Ali, and others (plates 1, 9-21). This iconography is strongly influenced by the Shiite doctrine of Islam,[22] for the Lebano-Syrian merchants to whom we owe the introduction and initial circulation of this imagery in Senegal were of Shiite persuasion.[23] Images of this kind are still reproduced today; they bring Koranic texts up to date, rendering them more accessible, even entertaining; ideological and didactic, these images are sometimes considered to be lucky charms, with owners investing them almost with the sacred character of the subjects they represent.

The subject-matter is rapidly broadened to include specifically African themes that are proper to Senegalese Moslem brotherhoods. The brotherhoods are mystical religious orders;[24] they originated in Sufism,[25] and they are differentiated by their teaching and their interpretation of the holy texts.[26] Each is headed by *marabouts*, or sheikhs (*sëriñ* in Wolof), with their own hierarchy, who serve as religious and spiritual leaders as well as diviners and magicians, and even, oddly enough, as businessmen.[27] Numerous reverse-glass paintings include portraits of

Fig. 10 Ibrahima Sall, *Noah's Ark*, 1992, 33 × 48 cm (10 × 19 in), private collection. In this work Noah is presented as a black person, as are Adam and Eve in Babacar Lo's painting.

the founders, and their successors, of the various brotherhoods, or provide narrative images of supreme moments in their lives. Certain subjects or decorative details include esoteric content that would at first only be perceived by followers. As for traditional Islam, the themes represented give the paintings an additional dimension – their mystical, propitiatory qualities. At the same time, these works can be objects of superstition and a means for propaganda. The images they convey are only the vehicles for ideas: their suggestiveness is intended to induce a straightforward, uncomplicated recognition. The qualities these works possess are supposed to be conceptual rather than formal, for the form is at the service of the content.

There are a number of religious brotherhoods in Senegal, but here we will restrict ourselves to four, the Mourides, the Tijaan, the Layen, and the Qadir. These are both the most important in terms of the size and influence of their followers, and those that have proved to be the most inspirational to artists.

The brotherhood of the Mourides[28] was founded by Sheikh Amadu Bamba (1850-1927), and it is affiliated to another great brotherhood, the Qadiriyya, which was originally founded in Iraq. Amadu Bamba followed the teachings of a Mauritanian Qadir *marabout*, and later founded the mosque at Touba, the holy place for all Mourides and the object of a yearly pilgrimage on the lines of those to Mecca. His conflicts with the French colonial administration made him famous and generated a whole series of stories concerning his life, the best-known one being his six-year exile in Gabon that began in 1896 (his teaching and his influence among Wolof aristocrats worried the French authorities enough to remove him from Senegal for a while).[29]

The imagery relating to Amadu Bamba is particularly rich, although all the portraits derive from a sole surviving photograph, which shows him standing up, dressed entirely in white, with his face half-hidden by a scarf (plate 22). The favourite themes are those that combine the supernatural with real-life incidents, including 'the prayer on the waves', 'the exile in Gabon' and 'the wandering of the *marabout*' (plates 23-34). Entangled in this iconography we can discern a systematic revival of themes drawn from traditional Islam: various miracles or great deeds by the Prophet, by his successors and by Arab saints are all revived and attributed to Amadu Bamba. Rather than being an encroachment, these revived incidents reveal ingenious forms of continuity, for, as a result, followers feel themselves to be on familiar ground. Events follow one another with a divine logic: Bamba, like Ali, fights the lion; like Mohammed he is guided, supported, inspired by Jibril (Gabriel) and the whole cohort of angels; like Mohammed and Ali he is confronted by monsters and *jinn*; like the Prophet and his successors he confronts the infidels; like the great saints of Islam he prays on the sea. The real-life story of Amadu Bamba reviewed and improved by his hagiographers is a true concentration of traditional Islam on Senegalese ground!

The brotherhood of the Tijaan (see plates 35-41) is a Wolof one. Founded by the Senegalese El Hadj Malick Sy (1855-1922), it stems from the Tijaniyya of North Africa, which has several branches.[30] Today in Senegal it continues to enjoy the greatest number of followers.[31] The

28 For the Mourides, see Cruise O'Brien, pp. 37-57; Diop, pp. 249-54; Monteil, 1966(a), pp. 160-68; Samb, 1972, pp. 423-33; Sy, pp. 428-32.

29 Of Tukulor origin, Sheikh Amadu Bamba was born in Mbake (named after his grandfather, Mballa Mbake), a village in the region of Baol, in the early 1850s (Monteil, 1966(a), p. 162, claims either 1851 or 1853; others, including Samb, 1972, p. 423, reckon the year of birth was 1855). His father, Momar Antasali, had settled in Cayor near the King (*damel*), Lat Dior, whose niece he married (this woman was not Bamba's mother, however). Following the King's death in 1886, Amadu Bamba returned to Baol and founded Touba (Monteil, 1966(a), p. 162). Initiated into Qadirism by his father, he continued his religious education in Mauritania, with Sheikh Sidiya Baba. During the years 1896-1902 he was in exile in Gabon, where he had been sent by the French colonial administration, who suspected he was fomenting a Holy War. Following his return to Senegal, he was once more exiled for the same reason, and spent the years 1903 to 1907 with his former master, Sidiya Baba, in Mauritania. He then spent five years under house arrest in the Department of Louga, after which he was allowed to settle at Diourbel, where he remained until his death in 1927. Here he continued to be closely supervised, though towards the end of his life he did in fact collaborate with the colonial administration. His tomb can be seen at the famous mosque at Touba.

30 El Hadj Malick Sy, like Sheikh Amadu Bamba, is of Tukulor origin, and both their brotherhoods were originally built up in Wolof areas (Marone, p. 140), which makes them essentially Wolof religious movements. Originally it appears that the Tijaniyya was a branch of the Quadir brotherhood, which Ahmed Tijani, the Maghrebi founder, simplified (Gouilly, pp. 108-10). One of the famous branches of the Tijaniyya of western Africa is that of the nineteenth-century Fulbe warrior *marabout*, El Hadj Omar, who lived in the region of Futa-Tora and in Mali (Diop, pp. 232-33; Marone, pp. 144-5; Samb, 1972, p. 331). In 1881 Malick Sy made the pilgrimage to Mecca, which bestowed on him the title of El Hadj. Famous for his great devotion, he ran the country dispensing his teaching. From 1902 to 1922, the year of his death, he remained in Tivaouane, the holy place of the Tijaan who go every year on a pilgrimage to honour his tomb (Marone, pp. 148-9; Samb, 1972, pp. 331-3).

31 Diop, pp. 255-62.
32 Born in Yoff in 1843, Libasse Thiaw, later Limamu Laye, began life among the Lebu as a fisherman. Illiterate, he saw nothing in himself that suggested he was predisposed to become a brilliant preacher. In 1883, however, he received divine inspiration and proclaimed himself to be the new *mahdi*, or messiah (Gaudefroy-Demombynes, p. 410). From that day forward he began spreading his ideas, which included granting a greater place for women in the practice of Islam (Sylla, 1971, p. 592). This is particularly interesting when one considers that the local Lebu animistic cults, against which Limamu Laye fought, were largely directed by women (Sylla, 1968, p. 81). In 1887 he was arrested and imprisoned by the French who feared his influence, but lack of real evidence soon secured his release. He preached for 26 years, and following his death in 1929 his sons and grandson have continued his mission down to our own times: first Issa Laye, until 1949, followed by his brother Mandione Laye, who led the brotherhood until 1971, and finally El Hadj Seydina Issa Thiaw, the son of the latter (Silla, 1971, pp. 590-641).
33 Silla, 1968, pp. 79, 81.
34 Gaye & Silla, pp. 499-523.
35 It is important to note that it has been mainly under the influence of the Mauritanian *marabouts* that the Qadir have been able to develop their orthodoxy as it is known in Senegal, for originally this brotherhood was partial to ecstatic demonstrations (the whirling dervishes are affiliated to this order). The same results are achieved by the Mauritanian *marabouts*, but without gesticulations or yells, for they prefer a very dignified and modest means of communion with God (Gouilly, pp. 96-7).
36 Diop. pp. 253-62.
37 Strobel, pp. 25-6.

holy city of the Tijaan is Tivaouane, their place of pilgrimage. Portraits of the founder, his Maghrebi homologue (Ahmed Tijani, 1737-1815), and his successors are the favourite themes of reverse-glass paintings relating to this brotherhood. Only among the brotherhood of the Mourides can the same degree of interest in a founder's life be found. And as is the case for Amadu Bamba, every portrait of El Hadj Malick Sy is based on a single photograph, in which, standing in front of the mosque at Tivaouane, he holds an umbrella (plates 37, 38).

The brotherhood of the Layen was founded by Limamu Laye (1843-1919). It maintains no links with any superior Arab or Maghrebi organization, and its followers are almost exclusively drawn from the Lebu ethnic group, whose home is Cape Verde.[32] An entirely aboriginal brotherhood, it ignores anything with connections to *rab* (spirits) and to *tuur* (ancestors), including songs and dances and the *ndëp* possession cults.[33] The main themes in Layen reverse-glass paintings have mostly to do with portraits of the founder's successors: Issa Rohu Laye, son of Limamu Laye (plate 44), and Mandione Laye (plate 42), second caliph of the brotherhood. Directly associated with the imagery of this brotherhood are two symbols, the flower of the prickly pear tree and the 'ethereal phaeton' bird, whose black-and-white colours are reproduced on the brotherhood's turban (plate 43). Although Limamu Laye was also present at many extraordinary events (it is said that he witnessed or was the object of several miracles, that he was hunted by the French colonial administration, that he was in exile, and so forth[34]) a tradition of representing different episodes in his life never developed. Like El Hadj Malick Sy, but unlike Sheikh Amadu Bamba, Limamu Laye and his successors have only inspired portraits of great sobriety. For although all of these brotherhoods made a cult of their founders, only in the case of the Mourides do we encounter true visual delirium and beguiling theatrical settings.

The brotherhood of the Qadir is the most orthodox one,[35] and it has the least number of followers in Senegal.[36] Its name refers directly to its Moorish founder, Sheikh Sidiyya El Kebir, who was himself dependent on the 'mother brotherhood' of the Iraqi Abd El Qadir el Jilani, who lived from 1079 to 1116 (plate 47). No Senegalese mediated as leader of a new branch, as was the case with the Tijaniyya.[37] Amadu Bamba, for example, began by following the teaching of a Moorish Qadir *marabout*, but later founded his own brotherhood. And it is most often in association with the Mouride *marabout* that we can find a few representations that include associations with the Qadir (plate 45), and even those are restricted to portraits.

There are, too, without any specific reference to one or other of the brotherhoods, several representations showing the various founders gathered together as in one single family (plate 46). This indicates that the ultimate reference is always to traditional Islam, and indeed no painter, whatever his brotherhood, feels the slightest reservation about producing images for other orders. There may well be financial incentives at work here, but the fact remains that, above all, these artists produce within a strictly Moslem field. Other paintings include scenes of divination (plate 93) and the Koranic school (plate 89).

Profane genres and subjects

It is in the genre of historic figures and deeds that we find the great figures of the Senegalese past, mainly political leaders who became illustrious by virtue of their struggles against the French invader. The most popular are Lat Dior, the sovereign (*Damel*) of Cayor, and Alburi Ndiaye, the sovereign of Djolof and a relative of Lat Dior.[38] Kocc Barma, a seventeenth-century figure famous for his moral tales, also features as a worthy historic figure.[39] Apart from the pictures of Lat Dior on the battlefield (plate 48), however, they are represented in so stereotypal a fashion that it is often difficult to identify them. Some pictures are almost emblematic images – allegorical evocations of resistance against the oppressor, be it the French colonial administration with Lat Dior and Alburi Ndiaye, or a despotic king, stubborn and violent, in the case of Kocc Barma (plates 49-52). And even though the theme of the cunning hero, the clever and noble defender of cultural values, is everywhere encountered, we are often unsure as to whether we see this or that supporting character, for the symbols that in theory should allow us to distinguish them are so merged, strangely combined or cancelled out by others that many pictures appear impenetrable to the outsider.

A special theme also has its place here, that of slavery. It is special in that it does not feature in traditional images of reverse-glass painting. In the 1980s, on the initiative of Y. Dupré, administrator of the Regards Croisés association, Gora Mbengue (see p. 24) produced a series of works relating to slavery. Then in 1989-90 Mor Gueye (pp. 24-5) took over and created a series inspired by the same theme. Here, for the first time, we are presented with a dramatic subject handled gravely. This is unusual, for reverse-glass paintings tend to tackle all themes positively, if not always with humour. Whether the subject is Islam, where we encounter religious propaganda or a cult of the saints, history, in which the praise of national heroes is sung, or tales and proverbs, where the oral tradition is itself celebrated, there is not one reverse-glass painting that is not optimistic. Even in scenes of daily life, humour, sometimes mixed with cynicism, is brought to bear on theft, adultery, domestic conflict and other problems, large and small. After all, the end justifies the means: the moral message asserts itself almost by accident, with ease and never sententiously. We receive constant lessons in good spirits; then, suddenly, in a commissioned work on slavery we encounter drama. Reverse-glass paintings bluntly confront us with the brutal reality: torture (plate 54), chains (plate 55), babies thrown to crocodiles in front of their mothers (plate 56), distress (plate 59), the house of the slaves at Gorée, whose 'door of no return' requires no comment (plate 58). It is, of course, impossible to handle the issue of slavery with detachment. Attemps to generate laughter in order to avoid crying would be inexcusable. The fact, therefore, that traditional reverse-glass painting never alludes to this episode in Senegal's history is in no way surprising, for it would be a departure from the fundamentally optimistic inclination of this art. Interesting as further attempts to portray the history of slavery might be, this particular commission was intended to teach a lesson in tolerance in schools and cultural centres, and slavery remains a marginal trend.

Further, one must not forget that reverse-glass paintings were originally intended exclusively for Senegalese people – to define their religious affiliation, for example, or to educate, or to supply decorative scenes that would give an aesthetic touch to a home. What Senegalese would want to awaken such painful memories when, thanks to reverse-glass painting, he can instead proclaim his deepest beliefs, both religious and intellectual?

Senegal and Gambia were the first regions in western Africa from whence slaves were exported. This commerce, at its height in the 18th century, was encouraged by the kings of Kayor and Baol, who traded human merchandise for various products, especially guns (plate 57).[40] Wolof aristocrats and leading citizens did not need the impetus of this commerce to create their own reserves of slaves, who were already to hand under the caste system.[41] They did not have any scruples about systematically seizing individuals or groups that they could use for bartering (plate 53). As for the French, their insatiable demand for African labour sanctioned this state of affairs. The lure of profit did the rest, establishing a foul triangular system of commerce that was to prove to be difficult to abolish.

Among the scenes of daily life there are some that are clearly historical evocations but contain no precise reference, context or character. These are illustrations of life long ago, with clothes and hair in the old fashion (plates 68, 69). Others, however, are quite current, recalling daily life in cities and villages (plates 73, 88). Works that feature dance and music come under the category of daily life, as well as scenes of wrestling, fishing, the market, professional activities and agricultural or domestic work (plates 60-98). Many comic accounts of human dramas and situations are also to be found, from adultery to theft, which are mostly just as at home in this category as they are in the next, which deals with moral tales and proverbs (plates 99-105).

It is interesting to note that reverse-glass painting, an essentially urban art-form, draws an enormous part of its inspiration from traditional events in the rural world and from practices nowadays either obsolete or nearly so. Commissions from tourists in search of exotic scenes partly account for this, but, as the artists themselves have insisted, one realizes that these happen also to be their own favourite themes. Nostalgic evocations of old times, the need to preserve disappearing practices and attitudes, the pleasure of recalling the faded beauty of a one-time *diriyànke* (an elegant and imposing woman) – all these are part of the concerns of painters, and it is quite true that in this they are related to the *griot*, the oral bard.[42] Unlike the *griot*, however, a painter does not necessarily belong to the ethnic group or region he recalls. Most glass-painters are Wolof (although this is gradually changing), but the subjects of their paintings have the most diverse ethnic origins.[43] Although never a part of the Senegalese scene, even nomads with their dromedaries are to be found pictured in scenes of daily life (plates 144, 146). But they remain a special case, for apart from the traditional Islamic subjects that are not directly connected with the brotherhoods, a few portraits and occasional commissioned works, Senegalese reverse-glass painting is, above all, directed towards more authentic Senegalese matters.

38 Monteil, 1966 (b), pp. 616-20; Ndiaye Leyti, pp. 993-4.
39 Sylla, 1978, p. 80.
40 Searing, pp. 23, 28-38.
41 Monteil, 1966 (a), pp. 83-8.
42 The *griot* recalls the high deeds of the old heroes, narrates myths and legends and praises the glory of noble families. He is respected, but also feared, and his words can be influenced by his personal assessments of others and partly by the money people give him.
43 Boisdur, pp. 193-4.

Moral tales and proverbs have generated a whole spectrum of paintings, often dealt with humorously, and with certain characters treated with derision. There is no doubt that these pictures follow the same pedagogic purpose as the tales, sayings, riddles and other stories that are told at home by the fireside in the evening. When the women were out buying reverse-glass paintings to decorate their homes, they not only sought out examples that articulated their religious beliefs, but also ones that would show examples of good and bad behaviour to their children (plates 106-16).[44]

Portraits feature among the favourite subjects of reverse-glass painting. Most are based on photographs (plate 134), but on occasion the subject has actually posed for the painter. Others are rather generic representations, like the woman with the *libidor* (a Wolof corruption of the French *louis d'or*, the old 20-franc gold-piece). Although originally inspired by the portrait of a woman called Aba Segou, this popular theme (plate 122) is an image of the Wolof woman *par excellence*, but with a touch of nostalgia introduced, for this style of hair, jewels and clothes is no more to be found. There is also the family portrait, the mother with her child or children, faces with pronounced ethnic characteristics, such as the portrait of the Fulbe woman, and imaginary representations of long-deceased character types that are part of the history of Senegal, the *ceddo*, for example (warriors of the old Wolof kingdoms), and the so-called 'Senegalese infantry'.[45] We are literally confronted with glass postcards, full of exoticism and affectation, easy, eye-catching, and not without charm (plates 117-34). Mammals, birds and flowers of all kinds are also to be discovered in reverse-glass paintings; these have no purpose other than to be decorative (plates 135-8).

There are also discrete groups of works that do not correspond to any of the categories mentioned up until now. There are the copies of the Tintin album-covers, for example (plate 143), mostly aimed at tourists, but in which some Senegalese have recently shown interest, for whom it is a form of exoticism. Most painters, none the less, appear to have reservations about reproducing such subjects, and indicate that they much prefer to concentrate on authentic Senegalese themes. The representations of Mammy Wata, largely inspired by a German chromolithograph depicting a woman of Indian descent (fig. 11), are also marginal because, although they evoke a water-spirit that is known in Senegal, it is usually represented like the one whose haunt is the Gulf of Benin, a thousand miles away (plates 139-41). The desert scenes (plates 144, 146), exotic and eye-catching, are equally unconventional themes for Senegalese artists.

There is too, the figure of Christ, which appears in several reverse-glass paintings. Although far from common, this catholicity on the part of the artists is not surprising, for as mentioned earlier they frequently make forays, commissioned or otherwise, into the territories of one or other of the various brotherhoods. With Christ on the cross, however, we are definitely leaving the Moslem world of the Wolof (plate 145). The image of Mary appears as a last concession of Moslem imagery, but the crucified Jesus as the Son of God is a claim not recognized anywhere in the Koran.[46]

Fig. 11 Anonymous, *The Snake Charmer*, no date, 43 x 33 cm (17 x 13 in), private collection. This German chromolithograph seems to have been the source of inspiration for the figures of Mammy Wata.

44 Ndiaye, Kelountang, pp. 40-3.
45 The term 'Senegalese infantry' was coined to refer to all those soldiers from French West Africa enlisted (usually by force) to fight in foreign campaigns, in their case the Great War in Europe. Originally most of them were Senegalese, and survivors from the trenches can still be found today. They are proud of their contribution, but bitter that the French Government refuses to grant them pensions and other advantages enjoyed by their French counterparts.
46 Gaudefroy-Demombynes, pp. 253-4; *Encyclopaedia of Islam*, II, p. 525.

Composition, style and technique

The art of reverse-glass painting has been through a number of changes in the course of time. The most significant ones mainly relate to style and technique. From a compositional point of view, except for those painters who prefer to keep their distance from the artisan tradition, the stylistic trend has tended to stay close to the frozen attitude of the standard photographic pose.

In general, artists buy their glass in large sheets of 130x48 cm (51x19 in) and then have them cut into manageable pieces. The standard formats are 33x48 cm (13x19 in), 24x33 cm (9.5x13 in), and 12x17 cm (5x7 in); on occasions, one also finds examples of 48x65 cm (19x25.5 in). Among the younger artists there is a bias towards contriving and working on less conventional formats. The thickness of the glass varies from two to three mm, but here again younger practitioners are displaying a preference for thicker glass, sometimes up to 9 mm, so as to reinforce the solidity of their works. Fragility and transportation problems are naturally a cause for hesitation on the part of many potential buyers, even though this ephemeral aspect of reverse-glass painting ought perhaps to be part of its charm.

Initially, the colours used were made from plants, a method that was quickly superseded by the industrial paints found in hardware shops. Thinned down, these dry more quickly, as compared with oil paint in tubes, although a few artists do use the latter. Traditional reverse-glass paintings present colour without relief or gradation – large flat washes in pure colours, with intense blues for sky or sea, deep greens for grass, violent reds, plain yellows, and so on. But little by little, pastel tones appeared, then colours began to merge, skies and seas were shaded, touches of white were added to the flat spreads of colour to give the impression of relief. However, the leading characteristic remains the broad application and daring combination of pure colours.

Formerly, artists made the wooden frames for their works themselves; nowadays, they still handle the finishing but it has become much hastier. Once the painted glass has dried (often in the sun), a salvaged piece of cardboard equipped with string is applied on the back of the painting and stuck to the glass by means of paper tape. This method, although not very durable, has the advantage of being inexpensive and quick, which, in the commercial context of reverse-glass production, is of particular importance.

It must be underlined that it is not due to a lack of technical knowledge that many of these Senegalese painters pay no heed to perspective or relative proportions, for their purpose is to radically emphasize certain elements in order to actualize the thing or person represented. The arts of Africa have been grossly misunderstood in these matters. Let us not forget that the task of a traditional reverse-glass painter is to represent a symbol, a religious or social value. This is why it is not an issue that the themes represented are always the same. The artist does not seek innovation at any cost. He untiringly repeats himself, reproduces his oldest subjects on the glass a hundred times, just as one makes numerous photographic prints from one negative. Within these limits, dictated by a respect for tradition, the painter finds his compensation in changing the colours, using new patterns for the garments, or choosing different jewels for his women. Of course, many younger painters have chosen to break with tradition, and concentrate on making very neat compositions, respecting all the academic rules of drawing. Many of their productions are close to comic-strips. Unfortunately, in so doing they lose the expressive, straightforward quality that characterizes traditional reverse-glass painting. Yet humour, a quality that seems never to fail, time and again rescues the finished product from a cold and distant formalism. Naturally, one increasingly notices a real drop in the quality of production. Reverse-paintings are, after all, aimed mainly at tourists, who are keen on exotic images at low cost. One must not, therefore, confuse works by those who have seized the opportunity to make a living by producing mediocre works or by plagiarizing those by others, with the artists who sincerely defend an artistic patrimony while making occasional sacrifices as a result of the market's requirements.

Professional training

The few self-taught artists apart, most reverse-glass painters begin as apprentices to a well-known painter. During the few years that their training comprises, all their work belongs to the master who, alone, signs the paintings and has the right to sell them. The apprenticeship is free and the work accomplished is voluntary. At the outset, apprentices only perform a few simple colouring tasks (fig. 12). Little by little they complete the different steps in the production of a single work, until they make one entirely on their own. They are free to stop their training when they wish and are not compelled to follow any particular schedule of attendance. Both parties profit from the relationship: an apprentice

Fig. 12 One of Mbida's apprentices, January 1994.

relieves his master of the most fastidious and routine operations, while in exchange the master passes on his knowledge and skills. Strictly speaking, there is no formal teaching, little guidance even; there is only practice, habit and experience.

The art market

As has already been pointed out, reverse-glass paintings were originally produced for a Senegalese public. Between 1930 and 1960 it was possible to find works at absurdly low prices, after which the domestic market began to dissolve. Not until the end of the 1980s did the well-to-do of Dakar deign once more to grant some value to this kind of artistic expression: noticing that foreigners were spending large amounts to buy certain works, they realized that reverse-glass paintings might well be a good investment.

Originally, there were only two means of distribution, both of which are still in use: either the artist sold his works himself, or he released them at low prices to a retailer who then sold them in the street at whatever rate of profit he could achieve. Currently, however, reverse-glass painting can realize high prices, for art galleries and exhibitions have become involved. The artists do not always make a profit from these, and some have even been exploited: works can reach very high prices on the market, prices that are negotiated by their managers or unscrupulous intermediaries, and, ultimately, the artists no longer control the financial operations generated by their works. Certain galleries have signed exclusivity contracts with painters, some of whom–attracted by the guarantee of steady work and income–have not clearly understood that they have lost the right to manage their own production. They find themselves excluded from discussions on the organization of exhibits and the tours. Sometimes even the artist's address is impossible to obtain and he is thus deprived of any opportunity to make himself known beyond the closed circuit of the gallery. On the other hand, a real traffic in forgeries is taking place: the apprentices, their period of training barely finished, are solicited to produce copies of works by their 'teacher'. Some do not hesitate to steal or photocopy designs. There is an irony in all this: apprentices, having had *their* works signed by their master, then set up on their own and begin signing their own works with the name of their former master! Mbida (pp. 27-8) is definitely the greatest victim of this: at the Kermel market in Dakar, a favourite place for tourists to visit, there is now hardly a single painting to be found signed in his name that is authentic. Disillusioned, but partly responsible, for he has trained a very great number of apprentices, (to such a point that his house had become more of a production-line factory than a workshop), he eventually decided to restrict his apprentices to his own sons and nephews.

Some leading artists[47]

Gora Mbengue who died in 1988, is the artist through whom the West discovered Senegalese reverse-glass painting. Some years ago a few Frenchmen living in Senegal took care of him, his family and his career (some did it with disinterest, others did not); following the publication in 1984 of Renaudeau and Strobel's book, *Peinture sous verre du Sénégal*, and the organization of a few trips to, and exhibitions in, France, Gora Mbengue became the artist against whom all the others in the field were measured. At the time of his death, all the media efforts on his behalf had finally begun to bear fruit and the price of his works increased considerably. Born into a family of farmers in Tiadiaye in 1931, Gora Mbengue was Wolof, a Tijaan Moslem, and a *geer*.[48] He began to paint in 1954 in Kaolack, and then lived in the suburbs of Dakar and in Pikine, before settling on the island of Gorée. It is interesting to note that, unusually, this self-taught artist never traced designs or models, but always began directly on the glass, which makes each of his works a unique piece.[49] He exhibited several times in France and Senegal, as well as in the USA in 1983.[50]

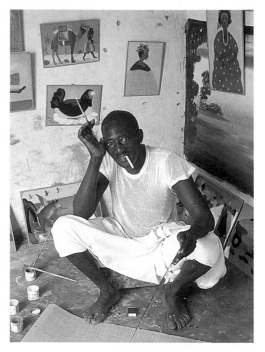

Gora Mbengue, June 1979.

'Through his glass-paintings, Gora confers on the painted thing his cultural memory, an expression of a tradition always present because always renewed, where all the affective energies of life are safeguarded. This childhood is buried in the depths of ourselves, but whose contact we need in order to withstand the servitude of the adult world. He thus assumes the duty of the painter, of the poet. The duty of the painter is in the gesture, in the motion, in the colour. It is thus that he impresses, it is thus that he expresses the luminous matter: from dreams to fantasies, from the known to the unknown, from the actual to the imaginary, from the metaphor to the essential. Unceasingly renewing the brilliant register of creation, always with the big astonished eyes of the "small prince".'[51] Gora's production, however, is of unequal quality. At times his work is less polished in the choice of colours, the quality of the ink lines and in the spreading of colours.

From an iconographic point of view, his works are very varied and handle all the themes mentioned earlier: Islam (plates 22, 23, 27, 28, 46) and non-traditional subjects (plates 140, 145) through to scenes that are decorative (plates 137, 138), historical (plates 48, 52-56, 59) or anecdotal (plates 81, 84, 88, 93, 103), and there are portraits too (plates 117, 119, 121). His work is characterized by his freedom from perspective, flat colouring, judicious and amusing disproportions and an unexpected mix of realism and imagination.

Mor Gueye a Wolof, Mouride Moslem and *geer*, was born in 1926 in the Department of Bambey. He began to paint while still living in his village, using paper as a medium and making his paints himself from plants. Around the age of 20 he discovered reverse-glass painting in Kaolack. At first he used the *calame* (the reed that is used for writing on Koranic boards) to draw his black outlines, and enamel paint. It was Gora Mbengue who initiated him, providing him with his first pen and introducing him to indian ink. During this period he used the wrapping

Mor Gueye, July 1993.

47 This book is not intended to provide an exhaustive coverage of all artists involved in the production of reverse-glass paintings. Our choice was dictated by subjective criteria and by material constraints. A number of artists could not be reached. Apart from the information on Gora Mbengue and a few other details in the text, the biographical information was gathered during research trips taken in 1993 and 1994 in Dakar, Rufisque and Thiès.

48 Wolof society was originally divided into castes, that is to say, into hierarchic, endogamous groups of hereditary professions. Nowadays, little attention is paid to this in the towns, although everyone knows to which caste he or she belongs, and as far as *geer* are concerned, they proclaim their own status loud and clear. Without entering into the details of this complex system, let us remark that there are two main castes: that superior to the *geer* and that of the *ñeeño* (craftsmen) (Diop, pp. 32-6; Silla, pp. 731-2). Given their handcraft activities, reverse-glass painters should belong to the caste of the *ñeeño*, but most of those we have mentioned are *geer*.

49 Boisdur, pp. 43-5; Renaudeau & Strobel, pp. 14-16; Strobel, pp. 16, 20.

50 Barbin, pp. 1-2.

51 Charles Carrere, excerpted from 'Gora-Cora-Gorée', a paper read at an evening on Senegal and Gora Mbengue, organized on 23 October 1989 at the Centre Georges Pompidou in Paris.

Babacar Lo and his wife, July 1993.

paper of Moroccan or Dutch sugar-loaves to create the drawings to be traced. He remained in Kaolack for two years, then, after various travels, ended up in Dakar on the eve of independence. He has remained settled in the centre of the capital since then, next to the court of the Moorish, and it is there that he pursues his career. He owns more than three hundred designs and works almost exclusively to order. The works that are signed 'Mor Gueye' are largely accomplished by his current apprentices, Samba Ndiaye and his son, Serigne Gueye. (Samba Ndiaye should be considered an employee rather than an apprentice, for he is paid for each reverse-glass painting he makes.) He generally uses glass 2 mm thick. For liquefying his paints he prefers to use petrol because thinner is 'bad for the health'. His favourite themes are religious scenes in relation to Mouridism (plates 25, 29), daily life (plates 82, 87) and portraits, especially of women with out of date hair-styles and jewels (plates 125, 132). He participated with Gora Mbengue in the creation of a series of paintings commemorating slavery (plates 57, 58). He is the only one who still makes reverse-glass paintings in black and white (plate 58). This approach might seem paradoxical since this kind of art attempts to emphasize the luminosity of colours under the transparency of the glass. However, when one examines the gradations from grey to black he manages to obtain, one realizes that it is still the same game of subtlety.

Babacar Lo a Wolof, Tijaan Moslem and *geer*, was born in 1929 in the Department of Bambey. He made his first reverse-glass paintings before the age of fifteen. Before that, he had started to sculpt but his father had opposed it, for the Moslem religion forbids all figural representations carried out in full relief.

Babacar Lo never had a master. At the outset of his career he mostly dedicated himself to religious themes, after which profane subjects began to feature (plates 31, 33, 35). Despite religion and although a Tijaan, he has always been eclectic and never hesitated to make paintings of stories belonging to other brotherhoods, notably all the episodes of Sheikh Amadu Bamba's life (plates 31, 33). In the late 1950s he practiced his art in Kaolack, after which he settled in Dakar, in Pikine, where he still lives. His workshop is prosperous. He has trained many apprentices but, at present, he works alone. His sons, one of whom is Moussa Lo (see pp. 30-1), and one of his three daughters, now deceased, learned the technique under him. Quite well known, he owes this both to the meticulousness of his work and to the consequence of the Western media interest that began with Gora Mbengue.

Babacar Lo also paints on canvas, which he admits is a technique that demands more time, more research and more personal involvement, but he does not disdain reverse-glass painting for all that. He works with or without 'pattern', but admits that with a design it is faster and easier to fulfil commissions. He adds, too, that even here he can give free range to his imagination in the arrangement of colours, the texture of garments, the quality of a gaze, the jewels, in short in all those details that account for the fact that two works based on the same design are at once so similar yet so different. He only works with enamel paint and indian ink; he buys primary colours and does his blending himself.

Above all, Babacar Lo enjoys subjects that come from stories of past times (plates 68, 69). Even when he paints a landscape he claims he is inspired by childhood memories. As far as profane themes are concerned, portraits are among his favourite subjects, especially women (plates 118, 122, 123). Dressing them, doing their hair, covering them with jewels, Babacar Lo finds some freedom while accommodating himself to the constraints caused by the technique in which he works. He always uses glass 2 mm thick, even for paintings of a larger format (plate 123).

Ibrahima Sall was born in 1939 in Lingeer, in the Department of Louga. A Wolof, Mouride Moslem and *geer*, he started to paint in 1956 with a master, Djiby Seck, with whom he remained for two years. In 1967 he started to sign his works; until then, his production had been 'anonymous'. Between 1972 and 1987 he followed another profession and painted only at weekends. Since 1987 painting has once more become his sole means of income. Although he lives in Rufisque, in the suburbs of Dakar, all his work is sold exclusively in the capital by an intermediary who takes a share and finds commissions. He has had several apprentices but, at present, is training only his young son, Mamadou Sall, a thirteen-year-old. He draws his models on paper or gains inspiration from a photograph or print. He works on several paintings at the same time (up to ten at once, according to demand). The process is begun when he first reproduces the drawing and puts the golden touches (gold powder mixed with thinner) on the glass. He then adds the various colours, one after the other, on up to three or four sheets of glass at once, for example adding yellow in every area of every work for which yellow is required. After drying, the same procedure is followed for subsequent colours. He liquefies his paint with petrol or cellulose thinner, which allows it to cover better and, above all, to dry faster. For the colour of black skin, he mixes black and red.

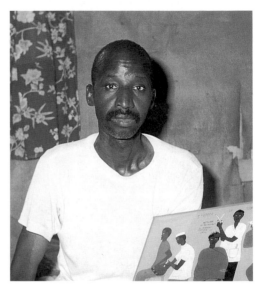

Ibrahima Sall, July 1993.

Ibrahima Sall's works are in the traditional style, both in technique (little or no perspective, disproportions to emphasize important details, flat colouring) and in subject-matter: religion, portraits and scenes of daily life (plates 49, 70, 76, 85, 102).

Magatte Ndiaye a Wolof and a Mouride Moslem, was born in 1940 in Gorée. His first artistic steps were taken under unusual circumstances: confined in the hospital at Fann, in the psychiatric wing, he was encouraged to paint in the 1970s by a French psychologist who provided him with all the equipment required to make reverse-glass works. Magatte Ndiaye's production now amounts to over two hundred designs on paper, all carefully numbered, with references to photographs of painted works so as to allow the customer to make his own choice. His paintings express the confusions of a sick man: malformed bodies, incandescent or blind gazes, surrealistic scenes. His favourite themes are women and the sun, which for him symbolizes masculine freedom. After his confinement in hospital Magatte returned to his home in Rufisque and continued painting. He used to take his results with him to Fann, to where each relapse in his mental condition unfailingly returned him. The social

Magatte Ndiaye, January 1994.

workers there acted as his sales agents. When we met him in January 1994, he had abandoned the creation of reverse-glass paintings because of a lack of funds and materials, but he was writing a good deal and drawing on the walls of houses. We therefore suggested that he take up painting once again and provided him with equipment, along with assistance from the painter Fode Camara, who is keen to encourage his talented compatriots. Plate 142 is an example of the results (see also plate 141).

Mbida, January 1994.

Mbida (his real name is Birahim Fall) was born in 1950 in the region of Thiès. Of Maurish-Bamana origins, he made his first reverse-glass paintings in 1972, having been working in other media for four years. He tried to introduce perspective and more correct proportions as well as gradations, but having realized that this did not fall within the traditional spirit of what is, after all, a popular art, he re-established the voluntary technical idiosyncrasies that give reverse-painting the unreal and symbolic qualities we know. None the less, concerned to add a personal hallmark and greater refinement and precision, he improved the shapes and softened the tints, judging the primary colours of traditional works to be too violent. This research led to him introducing the black background that emphasizes the harmony of colours and made him famous, above all among tourists. He explains that he used to use warm colours for his backgrounds until the day when, realizing that all African parties take place at night near the fireside, he decided to reproduce the atmosphere of the night: 'it is the African night, the negritude which, in spite of its blackness, is full of colour'. The leading artist of recent years, Mbida has endured the setbacks of his unexpected success, seeing himself pillaged, plagiarized, often clumsily copied, and exploited. He works with numerous apprentices, who perform a great deal of the work based on designs and whose professional activity pertains to 'artistic handicraft', to use an expression dear to him. For Mbida, untiringly copying on to the glass is a very banal activity, purely technical, and he compares himself to an engineer or an architect who conceives and supervises the execution of works but never lays down the bricks of his buildings. This situation has led him to want to create paintings of a different kind, unique, more abstract, made entirely by his own hand, directly on the glass, without passing through the stage of the traced model, pertaining to art rather than handicraft and thus more expensive. An erudite artist, Mbida explains his approach and his misfortunes with a distressing objectivity. He forbids himself to be trained by anyone. Although he worked with Modou Fall and Mor Gueye, he claims that their influence enabled him to detach himself from their manner. It was Gora Mbengue who helped him to improve his technique by giving him his first pen with which to draw the ink outlines. Until then he had been using a very thin brush. Mbida works with all kinds of paint, including enamel, gouache and oils. With gouache he uses a fixative and avoids superimposing the layers of colour in order to prevent their cracking. This variety in the choice of textures allows him to improve his performances, especially as far as mixes of colours are concerned, for which hardware paints do not suffice. The tints used for the background are generally mixed with petrol, while the others are mixed with thinner. For the colour of black skin he uses blue, red and a little white. He makes sure he slightly varies the carnations, to be realistic and to avoid the limbs of characters touching one another and becoming confused. To represent white people he mixes white, red and yellow in variable proportions. When applying the successive layers of colour, he starts with the white of the eyes and the gold of the jewels, then adds the flesh tint, then those of the garments. The thickness of his glass varies between 2 and 4 mm according to the size of the painting: Mbida attempts to have the least fragile finished products possible; the ephemeral charm of reverse-glass paintings means nothing to him. On the contrary, he is thinking of using mixes of glass and plexiglas to improve the solidity of his works, and of combining, in the elaboration of his paintings, all the materials traditionally used in Africa—wood, paper, fabric, canvas and so on. He has also made attempts at a 'natural perspective' by painting on several sheets that he then superimposes. He says that at the beginning of his career he particularly liked nudes, but having been violently criticized for this trend, he prefers now to exclude this subject from his repertory. The themes Mbida handles are very varied: portraits (plate 127), scenes of daily life (plates 72, 77, 100, 107), Koranic schools (plate 89). He has also created an impressive series of musicians: players of *balafon*, *kora*, *xalam*, *tama*, etc. (plates 61, 62, 64, 65).

Alexis Ngom born in 1957 in Fao, Department of Mbour, is Serer and a Moslem. His Serer name is Geej Ngom. He was baptised Alexis in 1964, then converted to Islam in 1973. His Moslem name is Lamine. He started his painting career as an apprentice under Gora Mbengue from 1975 to 1977. In 1978 he started to work alone, but only in 1979 did he get his first workshop. Customers generally go directly to him and place their orders by looking at photographs of his works in the albums he continues to compile. He no longer uses intermediaries to sell his production, and the Bigue Ndoye Gallery is one of the rare places where it is still possible to find examples of his work. Meticulous and respectful of his commitments, he accomplishes his work alone, within the agreed deadlines. When the demands of his many orders leave him time to relax he applies himself to perfecting his art, creating new designs and researching new mixes of colour. He also works on several paintings at the same time, first on the drawing in indian ink, then on the colouring. He always begins by applying the lighter colours and adds volume with touches of white that blend into the basic tint. With Alexis, ink outlines no longer confine colours; they can be shaded, blended, modulated between these limits. He dilutes his paintings only with petrol and only uses glass 2 mm thick. When making portraits, he often turns to photographs. He sometimes creates directly on the glass and, if the result pleases him, then photographs it and copies it as a drawing on paper. Like Babacar Lo, he manages to work quite well within the constraints of the techniques of reverse-glass painting, and gives free range to his imagination in the way he treats the garments, the jewels and the colours. His very particular style combines his arrangements of geometrical shapes, such as the triangles of the *boubous* (plates 126, 131),[52] with an eye for detail and very

52 The *boubou* is a wide garment that falls to the feet. Worn both by men and women, it comprises a large piece of cloth at the centre of which is a hole for the head. It is generally richly embroidered around the neck and on the great ventral pocket stitched to the ones men wear. For men, the *boubou* is one of the three pieces of a costume called *ñett abdu* in Wolof (three Abdu) in reference to three famous *marabouts* from different brotherhoods: El Hadj Abdu Sy, a Tijaan, present caliph of Dakar, Abd El Qadir El Jilani, a Qadir, and Abdul Lahad Mbake, a Mouride. The other two parts of this three-piece suit are the *caaya* (see plate 25) and the *jam put* (which pricks the throat), a shirt with a neck opening that comes to a point at the Adam's apple.

53 The ENDA-Tiers Monde is an association based in Dakar that devotes itself to Third World problems regarding environmental issues and economic development.

54 Bouttiaux-Ndiaye, p. 39; Ndiaye, Keloun-tang, pp. 42-3.

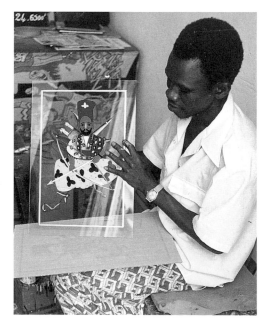

Alexis Ngom, July 1993.

surprising blends of colour. His work is paradoxically simple and sophisticated. Sometimes close to caricature, he can express motion in a few incisive lines (plate 104), or on the contrary, produce figures of stone. We find fugacity, rapidity and humour in the scenes recalling proverbs or sayings (plates 110, 111, 113, 114); stillness, fixity and permanence in the portraits (plates 126, 131).

Mallos, January 1994.

Mallos was born Maleyni Sow in Dakar in 1958. He is Fulbe and a Qadir Moslem. First trained in publicity drawing, he has been working as an artist since 1973. Until 1982 he was in conflict with his family, who opposed his career (his father, a policeman, wished to see him follow the same path). But since then his work as an artist has enabled him to provide for his family, and they no longer have the slightest objection to it. In 1986 he took up reverse-glass painting, creating pictures with Christian themes for the Church of Notre-Dame in Pikine. Like most of his fellow artists, he works to order. He too has noticed that Senegalese people are once more buying reverse-glass painting, and that they are particularly interested in scenes of daily life and subjects relating to *cosaan* (origins, traditions). Mallos is mostly known for his series of works on professions and health (plate 95), which are treated in the manner of comic-books. He created the first painting of this kind in 1989 as a project for a competition organized by the ENDA-Tiers Monde association[53] on the theme of AIDS.[54] Prior to December 1993 he used retailers to sell his works; since then he has obtained a space at the Kermel market, where he has a stall he can manage for himself (see also plate 124).

Azu Bade, January 1994.

Azu Bade born Amadu Seck in 1958 in St-Louis, is Wolof and a Tijaan Moslem. He took up reverse-glass painting in 1988. He was previously trained (1982-86) as a tailor and ran his own sewing workshop. All that he earned he invested in painting materials. He registered at the School of Fine Arts in the communication department and left in 1992 with a certificate in graphic design. He now works as a fashion designer, graphic designer, and reverse-glass painter. At present he no longer uses intermediaries to sell on the street for he says that it is 'more profitable to the retailer than to the artist'. He wishes to concentrate on preparing works for exhibition in art galleries. He abandoned the naive trend that is widely followed at present, refuses to work with flat colouring, and wants to make use of his experience and skills as a graphic designer. His favourite theme is daily life, he shows little interest in religious themes and sometimes attempts to introduce a critical view, a humorous note or a message in his works (plates 101, 105). He also uses designs on paper, which he then traces and, like many others, finds great satisfaction in changing his colours according to the mood of the moment (see also plate 86).

Paco Diagne was born in 1965 in Dakar. He is Wolof and lives in the neighbourhood of the Medina. He started using the technique of reverse-glass painting in 1990, influenced by his brother Metzo, who was then training under Mbida. His artistic career, however, began in 1980 with painting on canvas and pictures made with sands of different colours. He varies the format of his glass and he also sometimes suppresses the ink lines in certain areas of some works. He then takes advantage of these inkless parts, notably in landscapes, to play with colour gradations (plate 146). He often works from a design drawn on paper, which he carefully traces. He is both very meticulous and audacious in the drawing and in the treatment of colours when they are not defined by the ink outlines. It is interesting to note that all the parts outlined in ink are properly filled with flat tints, while the rest of the glass can be the ground of mixes, combinations and blendings of tints, as if the ink lines had the effect of imprisoning the colours, forbidding them contact with other shades. Through these details we can see that Paco's works are like him – ambitious, thoughtful, provocative and disciplined. He hesitates to use the usual circuit of retailers or other middle-men to sell his works, preferring to show them in galleries. For the time being, reverse-glass paintings do not provide him with a sufficient income, and thus he also works as a carpenter with his father (see plate 63).

Paco, July 1993.

Metzo says Ahmad Diagne (his real name) was born in 1967. He is Wolof and works with his brother, Paco, in the neighbourhood of the Medina in Dakar. For three years (1989-92) he worked as an apprentice under Mbida. Painting is his sole professional activity. He makes sophisticated drawings on glass, which are almost self-sufficient, after which the application of colours is almost anecdotal without being superfluous. He has banished gold from his painting, which, in his opinion, is too much in the manner of Mbida. Aware of the great wave of plagiarism from which Mbida's works suffer, Metzo wanted to keep his distance at all costs and decided to carry out his own research by exploring new paths in the field. He tackles this together with his brother. Metzo wants his paintings to be beautiful, pleasant and agreeable. He very much insists on this, adding that, even if he is sad, he concentrates all his efforts on not showing it. In fact, while harmony and serenity emanate from his works, there is melancholy too. For, contrary to his aspirations, Metzo has not been able to banish the 'blue notes' from his works, revealed in his choice of colours – blue, violet and mauve. Although he certainly does not have the audacity of his brother, Paco does not have his tenderness. The two of them have abandoned the usual formats of the medium but they both achieve subtle and delicate associations and blendings of colour, and despite their exotic subjects, both of them still remain traditional reverse-glass painters (see plates 128-30).

Moussa Lo a Wolof, Tijaan Moslem and *geer*, was born in 1971 in Kaolack. He started to paint at the age of ten. In 1984 he learned the technique of reverse-glass painting from his father, Babacar Lo, at whose side he worked for one year. During this training period he copied his father's drawings and then made paintings on the basis of them. In 1985 he set up his own workshop (in his mother's house, Babacar Lo's first wife) and started creating new designs. Moussa Lo has already trained two apprentices, one of whom, Yacouba Ndiaye, his cousin, is currently working with him. Reverse-glass painting is not his sole means of subsistence, for he is also a percussionist and dancer, which means he is

Metzo, July 1993.

Moussa Lo, July 1993.

Cheikh Ndao, July 1993.

55 The Laobe, or Lawbe, are the endogamous caste of sculptors of Fulbe ethnic origin (Diop, p. 50).

often away on tour. His approach as a painter, completely in the traditional style, remains very classical, without surprises or novelty. The influence of Babacar Lo in the quality and precision of the drawing is obvious. Given his youth it is perhaps surprising that he is so conventional. Once he had fully mastered his art, one might have expected greater innovation to follow. However, Moussa Lo has chosen to maintain the tradition in the manner of his elders. He thins down his paints with petrol and uses cellulose thinner only for the gold. To render black skin he mixes black, yellow, red and a little white; for white skin he uses red, brown and white. His paintings are sold in the Kermel market, and in the workshop of Mor Gueye (see plates 60, 96, 120).

Cheikh Ndao was born in 1975 in Dakar. A Wolof, he worked for three years (1990-93) as an apprentice under Mbida; only in April 1993 did he set up on his own. His father, a schoolteacher, was encouraging, and lent him the initial funds to purchase the materials. This young, talented artist sits at the border between traditional popular reverse-glass painting and more erudite forms of contemporary painting. Starting from conventional themes, he has created a new style of emotion expressed in his most abstract works. Some of these paintings are totally non-figurative; others are partly so, and show a drawing in ink drowned in spurts of colour. This ink line increasingly tends to disappear in almost totally abstract pieces; it is like a last nod to popular art. Cheikh Ndao works only with thinner, for petrol takes longer to dry. He uses enamel colours and gouaches. He is also fiercely making a point of breaking away from Mbida's ascendancy, not because he does not value his work, but rather because he is solicited by unscrupulous gallery owners who ask him to make forgeries, as are other former apprentices. Fortunately, some dealers have already perceived the talent of this newcomer on the scene. At the Anthéna gallery, among others, some of his beautiful productions can be found. The works of Cheikh Ndao that are sold on the street are of lesser quality. He is definitely an artist with a great future, although he still lacks experience, practice and the means of establishing himself for good as a 'scholarly' contemporary painter (see plates 66, 67).

The workshop of the Museum of Thiès

The Museum of Thiès maintains a workshop for artists who, since 1988, have specialized in reverse-glass painting. This workshop depends on a cultural centre established at the same location as the Museum, and it is thanks to this that a working space has been placed at the disposal of young artists.

Arona Diarra was born in Thiès in 1950; he is Bambara and a Mouride Moslem. He started to paint at the age of eighteen. Self-taught, he nevertheless benefited from the counsel of friends teaching at Dakar's School of Arts. They gave him a few ideas concerning anatomy and perspective and thus allowed him to make rapid progress. He made several attempts in sculpture but was dissuaded from continuing, for this is an activity reserved for the Laobe[55] and forbidden by Islam. He started reverse-glass painting in 1988, almost by chance, to help his friend Mbida who, based in Dakar, had received an order for 200 paintings to be done in no time and which he could not complete on his own. Arona Diarra came to like this technique but hesitated to put it into practice in Thiès, thinking that it had no future in such a small town. But having followed the advice of Mbida, who encouraged him to progress in this way, he rapidly realized that he sold more glass than canvas paintings. Installed as head of the workshop at the Museum from 1978 to 1991, he has trained many apprentices in this new technique. Together they have received a few big commissions from various hotels. Since 1991 Arona Diarra has been employed at the Aldiana Club in Mbour (a holiday resort for European tourists, mainly Germans), where he takes care of the decoration workshop. He creates theatre sets for dramatic productions and runs discos. The club's shop displays reverse-glass paintings, often of mediocre quality, but not a single one by this talented painter who is on the spot 24 hours a day, suffers from no longer being able to practise his art, ready as he is to offer his services, and who could benefit financially. He must wait for the weekends to return to his workshop at Thiès. Scenes of daily life (plates 79, 92) and religious themes (plates 26, 75) feature among his favourites. He also confirms the fact that the Senegalese have started again to show some interest in this traditional art-form, notably some Moslems who commission scenes on subjects that relate to the various brotherhoods.

Arona Diarra, January 1994.

Moussa Johnson was born in 1953 in St-Louis. His family originates from Sierra Leone. He is a Moslem, but is not a member of a specific brotherhood. Self-taught, he began with reverse-glass painting in 1980 in St-Louis, probably inspired by the numerous paintings owned by his grandmother. He arrived in Thiès in 1983, where he worked with Arona Diarra. His favourite themes are scenes of daily life that contain humour. He works essentially to order; on occasions, therefore, he also handles

Moussa Johnson, January 1994.

Jules, January 1994.

Gabou, January 1994.

religious subjects. He participated along with 46 other African and European artists in the 'Hé! bonjour Monsieur La Fontaine' exhibition dedicated to La Fontaine's *Fables*, for which he prepared four paintings: *The Wolf and the Lamb*, *The Old Lion*, *The Crow and the Fox* and *The Cock and the Fox*.[56] Moussa Johnson sometimes works directly on the glass but generally uses designs, which he then traces. He also makes frames out of straw (see plates 71, 80). He has one apprentice, Mamadou Ndiaye Faye, who has been working with him for four years and who is now beginning to sign his own works.

Jules   (Souleymane Dione) was born in 1958 in Dakar, the offspring of a Serer father and a Bambara mother. He has been painting on canvas and on paper since 1982 and on glass since 1990. Having lived in Thiès since 1963, he entered the Museum in 1990, after having been employed by a company involved in rural development. Since then he has dedicated himself to painting. He was trained in the technique of reverse-glass painting by Arona Diarra. Jules almost never works to order; he prepares his paintings, then exhibits them at the Museum, where they are mostly bought by passing tourists. His favourite themes are scenes of daily life and solely decorative subjects. He works a lot on nudes but encounters opposition to this subject because of Islam. At the Museum he also manages the sale of Diarra's works while the former fulfils his contract in the holiday resort of Mbour (see plates 78, 98).

Gabou   born Gabriel Balacoune in Dakar in 1965, is Mancagne and a Christian. He has been painting since 1987. In 1988 he became Mbida's apprentice and followed his training in Dakar. In 1992 he opened his own workshop after having spent three years at the Museum of Thiès. He has two apprentices, Habib Ba and Vieux Biramou Coumaré. He mainly produces paintings on Catholic religious themes, which he sells every year in Popenguine, where a famous Christian pilgrimage takes place. His scenes of daily life are handled with a lot of humour (plates 73, 74, 94, 99). There is almost always a rascally aspect to his paintings, often personified in a voyeur who takes advantage of every situation. He also paints nudes which, in traditional reverse-glass painting, is a true revolution (plate 94). He has a very personal style, a lot of verve and taste, and is largely independent of Mbida's influence. He sells his paintings in Dakar, in a gallery on Mohammed V Street, which regularly arranges commissions for him. His apprentices have already mastered quite well the various stages of the making of a reverse-glass painting and, on occasion, Gabou gladly lets them produce works of their own that they can sell at the Museum.

Khaly   (Papa Khaly Diop) was born in Thiès in 1969; he is Wolof and a Tijaan Moslem. He began reverse-glass painting in 1989 with Arona Diarra. To dedicate himself fully to his new passion, he abandoned his studies. On the advice of his master, he first acquired the mastery of the technique of making designs on paper, creating new subjects and developing others. Later, he was asked to put down the colours on the net of ink outlines that Diarra had reproduced on the glass. This apprentice-

Khaly, January 1994.

ship, which lasted for two-and-a-half years, allowed him to master progressively all the stages of the creation of a work. Daily life is his favourite theme. He says that all the situations he witnesses, in the village or in the city, are potential subjects for him. He continually observes with the painter's eye, sketches on the spot or later reproduces the scene at the Museum's workshop. Several of his works deal with a delicate subject concerning *marabouts* and the young children in their charge, for some *marabouts* are not always capable of assuming this responsibility fully (plates 90, 91). Khaly insists on the fact that he cannot answer for the dealings of those *marabouts* who abuse their power and thus contravene the precepts of the Moslem religion. He mostly works for tourists and thus produces relatively few paintings on religious themes. He participated with Moussa Johnson in the exhibition on the *Fables* of La Fontaine, to which he contributed three works: *The Crow and the Fox*, *The Thief and the Donkey* (plate 106) and *The Fox Pleading against the Wolf in front of the Monkey*.

Other contemporary artists

One cannot pass over in silence the various contemporary Senegalese painters who have recovered the technique of reverse-glass painting in order to achieve their own artistic goals. Among them is Serigne Ndiaye who is very well aware of the whole problem of traditional reverse-glass paintings. He collects them and has also written on the subject.[57] A very well-known painter in Senegal, he exhibited in Dakar (June 1993) a series of works entitled 'The Aristo'. These are portraits of Fulbe men and women, a traditional theme, but here treated quite differently (plate 149).

Sea Diallo also produces interesting work by combining the techniques of reverse-glass painting and collage. An artist of great talent, he states that he cannot dedicate himself solely to traditional glass painting, for this means constantly recopying the same designs, a practice that leaves him totally frustrated. The small amount of creative freedom there is to be found in colouring is of no help to him: for him each painting is the result of research on shapes, materials, tints. Moreover, he could never stand the thematic limitations to which most artists of the traditional technique have to conform if they do not want to be criticised. In some of his recent works he has used paints he made himself on the basis of vegetable pigments: green and red sorrel, henna, coffee. A recurrent theme for Sea is the woman, captivating, almost disquieting (plate 150). Fantasies, frustrations and anxieties – a very life-like painting.

Hassane Sar is also a young artist who works in this way. Like Serigne Ndiaye and Sea Diallo, his work mostly consists of glass paintings. A graduate of the School of Fine Arts (1993), he also makes furniture, which he ornaments with pieces of coloured glass. For his paintings he begins with the shapes and patterns of his materials – car windscreens and broken glass, for example, the aesthetic qualities of whose cracks he exploits (plate 148). A close friend of Azu Bade, he understands the

57 Ndiaye, Serigne, pp. 165-8.
58 This was exhibited at the 8F Gallery, Dakar, December 1993-January 1994.

problems of traditional reverse-glass painting quite well, and, aware of its contraints, has deliberately chosen a way of working that leaves him more freedom.

Two other well-known artists should also be mentioned, despite the fact that glass painting is not their speciality: Souleymane Keita and Amadou Sow. Living on the island of Gorée, Souleymane Keita has painted on glass by way of experiment. He has nevertheless produced some works of quality, in which he combines scraping on the front and back of the glass with oil painting on the back. As for Amadou Sow, now living in Vienna, he has just presented in Dakar a fascinating exhibition of plexiglas painted with acrylic.[58] He thus uses the same traditional method of painting on the reverse of a transparent medium but with a fundamentally different aim, that is to create works that endure (plate 147). We have seen that Mbida, worried by the fragility of glass, has sought to strengthen his works. Amadou Sow, also concerned to offer paintings that do not destruct as soon as they are moved, has solved the problem by using plexiglas.

Conclusion

The evolution of reverse-glass painting in Senegal has enabled us to witness both a progressive diversification of the subjects handled, and the fact that, through the Wolof, it has become fully Senegalese. As a matter of fact, young people who practice this art nowadays are of various ethnic origins, as well as of different religious persuasions, which has taken this art-form away from its original close relationship with Islam. On the other hand, the more we progress in the study of it, the more we realize how undefined is the gap between scholarly and popular art, for there is always a moment, hard to grasp, where one becomes the other. In our account we have attempted to present a popular art, one that offers itself as a subject of study both from the artistic point of view and from those of history, ethnography, even linguistics. Popular works are still too much neglected by art historians. Reverse-glass painting is often criticised because it largely depends on countless works based on a single design; no one, however, claimed that art-photographers were not really artistic because they made several prints from one negative! In addition, the technique employed for reverse-glass painting at least makes something different of each 'impression', something thought and felt at the time of its creation! We must admit that this kind of art first attracted our anthropological interest – fabulous subjects that allowed us to approach a culture through its images. It is only later that we reacted artistically to the freshness of the subjects, the qualities of the compositions, the chromatic games, the dimension contributed by light through the transparency of the glass, the powerful expressiveness of these works. An intellectual advance and a beautiful lesson in modesty. May it so serve others.

PLATES

1

Anonymous

Al Boraq, no date
chromolithograph, with a painted
background
50 x 61 cm (20 x 24 in)
Private collection

A rare example of the chromolithographs
that were forbidden by the French colonial
administration, and which, as a result, were
traced onto glass. This, of course, in turn
led to the development of reverse-glass
painting. In the example shown here, however, the original chromolithograph that
depicts Al Boraq, the winged mount of
the prophet Mohammed, is pasted on the
reverse of the glass, onto which a painted
ornamental composition of peacocks and
flowers has been added.

2

Anonymous

Seated Man, no date

photograph, with a painted decorative
background
50 x 60 cm (20 x 23.5 in)
Royal Museum of Central Africa, Tervuren

A portrait photograph of an unknown man
pasted on the back of the glass, to which a
painted background of peacocks and stands
of flowers has been added. The inclusion of
birds shown back to back, and flowers, is
the result of Western influence, for neither
filling homes with plants nor giving flowers
as gifts are Senegalese traditions.

3

Anonymous

Two Seated Women, no date

photograph, with a painted decorative
background, 50 x 50 cm (20 x 20 in)
Private collection

A portrait photograph of two unidentified women has been decorated with a painting of facing birds and potted, flowering plants. Photographs of this kind yield precious information on the garments and hairstyles favoured in Senegal earlier this century, here perhaps of the period 1925-30 ('Souweres', p. 16). To portray figures in a manner akin to formal photographs of this sort was to become one of the favourite modes of presentation in reverse-glass painting.

4
Anonymous
A Young Woman, no date
photograph, with a painted decorative
background, 45 x 47 cm (17.5 x 18.5 in)
Royal Museum of Central Africa, Tervuren

A portrait photograph decorated with
peacocks and flowering plants.

5
Anonymous
Facing Parrots, no date
41 x 58 cm (16 x 23 in)
Private collection

Placed either side of a floral composition,
the birds derive from characters that form a
Koranic verse, that is, the calligraphy has
been shaped into parrot-like forms.

6
Anonymous
Mosque, no date
60 x 50 cm (23.5 x 20 in).
Private collection

This mosque is probably the one at Medina.
Beneath the dome the arcaded inner court
is presented on a flat plane, without perspective. At the apex of the composition can be
seen the star and crescent of Islam.

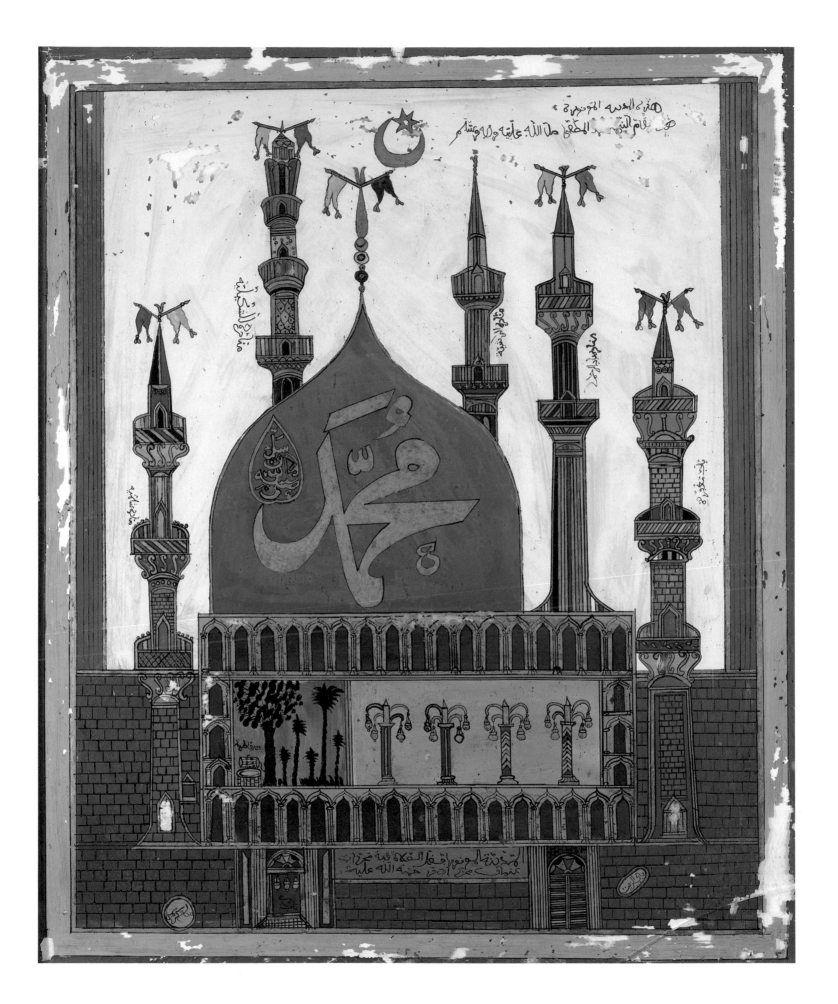

7

Anonymous

Nativity, no date

30 x 40 cm (12 x 16 in)
Private collection

The Koran, of course, borrows numerous themes
and episodes from the Bible, although most are
from the Old Testament. In this example, the scene
is the New Testament one of the birth of Jesus,
for Mary herself is a respected figure in the Moslem
tradition (Gaudefroy-Demombynes, pp. 100, 235-6).

8

Anonymous

The Sacrifice of Abraham, no date

32 x 33 cm (12,5 x 13 in)
Royal Museum of Central Africa, Tervuren

This episode from the Old Testament is frequently represented in reverse-glass painting; here the angel interrupts Abraham, who is about to slit the throat of Isaac, his own son, and offers him a sheep as a substitute. For the Moslems the feast of the sheep, called Tabaski by the Senegalese, is a reminder of Abraham's exemplary commitment to God.

9

Anonymous
Al Boraq Flying over Mecca, no date
40 x 50 cm (16 x 20 in)
Private collection

Al Boraq is the winged mount of the Prophet Mohammed. According to a legendary tale revived in the Koran, the angel Jibril (Gabriel) sought out Mohammed and gave him a mount with a woman's head on which Mohammed then went from Mecca to Jerusalem, after which he travelled the seven skies (Gaudefroy-Demombynes, pp. 92-4). In the Wolof language, Al Boraq's speed is described as being as quick as a wink (*xef ak xippi*) or as fast as the mind: *xel bi dem, bët gis ko, tank teggü fa* (the mind thinks of it, the eye sees, and the foot then rests there). In 1911 William Ponty (see notes 14 and 15) considered that the images of Al Boraq were propagandist, alluding to the apotheosis of Islam. This painting is of particular interest because Mohammed is actually shown in person. Usually, the representation of Al Boraq alone suffices to remind a believer of the miraculous night of the *miraj* (the ascension to heaven).

10
Anonymous
Al Boraq, no date
33 x 43 cm (13 x 17 in)
Private collection

11
Anonymous
The Hegira, no date
37 x 50 cm (15 x 20 in)
Private collection

This scene, Mohammed's flight from Mecca to Medina in 622, marks
the beginning of a new era, year 1 in the Moslem calendar. Mohammed and his companion, Abu Bakr, are attempting to escape from
their pursuers. Allah comes to their rescue by sending a pigeon,
seen here making its nest, and a spider, which spins its web across
the entrance of the cave in which Mohammed and Abu Bakr have
hidden themselves. For easier comprehension, the artist here chose
to show Mohammed and Abu Bakr running towards a cave that already features the web the spider actually spins after they have hidden themselves away. Thus, we see a sequential narrative collected
in a single image – the fugitives running towards the cave, and the
cave after they have been protectively sealed within it by the spider.

12
Anonymous
The Torments of the Damned, no date
Private collection

Here sinners, after death, are subjected to
divine justice, receiving punishments in pro-
portion to the degree of their bad actions
during life. The *malaïka* (angels) are responsible for delivering just punishment;
here they resemble Anubis and Thoth, two
Egyptian gods. Anubis, the jackal-headed
god, is an embalmer who conducts souls to
the place of the dead, while Thoth, the ibis-
or baboon-headed god, serves as a scribe,
keeping a record of the deceased (Drioton &
Vandier, pp. 66-7, 71, 75; Erman, pp. 61-2,
65-6).

13

Anonymous
The Battle of Badr, no date
51 x 120 cm (20 x 47 in)
Royal Museum of Central Africa, Tervuren

The Battle of Badr in 624 saw the defeat of the Koreishites, who had settled at Mecca, by the followers of Mohammed. This victory generated a series of legendary tales that claimed the victory was due to divine intervention: Allah sent the angels, *malaïka*, to lend the prophet a helping hand by hurling down stones on the enemy who carries the banner with a profile of a human face. Mo-

hammed can be seen astride Al Boraq in the centre of the composition. His followers (one of whom carries the banner with its crescent and stars) include the four caliphs, his successors: Abu Bakr, Omar, Othman and Ali. The inscriptions in Arabic and in Wolofal (i.e., Wolof transcribed in Arabic) identify the various caliphs and angels. Bilal, the first of the muezzins (those that call the faithful to prayer), is also featured, here beating a drum at the foot of a palm-tree (*Encyclopaedia of Islam*, I, p. 559; Gaudefroy-Demombynes, pp. 119-23, 472; Renaudeau & Strobel, pp. 44-5; 'Souweres', p. 21; Strobel, p. 49).

14

Anonymous

Ali and his Sons, no date

54 x 60 cm (21 x 23.5 in)
Private collection

Ali, the Prophet's cousin, became his son-in-law when he married Mohammed's daughter, Fatima. Ali was the fourth caliph of Islam and the founder of the Shiite doctrine (see note 22). He is represented here with his two sons, Hasan and Husayn (*Encyclopaedia of Islam*, I, pp. 283-5; Gaudefroy-Demombynes, pp. 129, 236-8).

15

Anonymous
The Four Caliphs and Bilal,
no date
48×64 cm (19×25 in)
Royal Museum of Central Africa, Tervuren

Abu Bakr, Omar, Othman and Ali appear on horseback, while, far left, is Bilal. They have gathered at the tomb of Hamza (Mohammed's uncle), who died at the Battle of Ohod in 625. (During this battle, the Koreishites of Mecca gained some revenge on Mohammed's followers: the texts indicate that as many Moslems died at Ohod as had Koreishites at the Battle of Badr the previous year.) Whereas the victory at Badr is celebrated in a depiction of the combat (see pl. 13), the image of the Prophet's four companions at Hamza's grave refers to the disastrous failure at Ohod. Bilal, who is also included here, was an Abyssinian slave attached to Mohammed. When the Prophet died, he was set free in Medina by Abu Bakr (the first caliph, Mohammed's successor). This black slave who fought on the Moslem side was one of the first such followers of Islam, and is celebrated by African Moslems as their chief ancestor, hence his frequent inclusion by Senegalese artists in their depictions of Islam's founding fathers (*Encyclopaedia of Islam*, I, pp. 718-9; II, pp. 254-5; Strobel, pp. 35-7).

16

Anonymous

Ali's Fight with the Lion, no date

39 x 46 cm (15 x 18 in)

Private collection

Ali, famous both for his piety and his bravery, took part in numerous battles on the Prophet's side. His courage is here celebrated in the legendary story of his struggle to overcome a savage lion.

17

Anonymous

Ali's Fight with Amr, no date

45 x 49 cm (18 x 19 in)

Private collection

Another evocation of Ali as a fervent defender of Islam, in this case in combat with the infidel Amr. Here Ali has severed Amr's leg, which Amr brandishes in his final attempt to overcome Ali. This confrontation appears to have taken place during the Battle of the Ditch in the year 626, in which, once again, the Koreishites fought against the Moslems (Gaudefroy-Demombynes, pp. 140-42; Strobel, p. 45).

18

Anonymous

Abu Bakr and Omar, no date

45 x 50 cm (18 x 20 in)
Private collection

Depicted here are the first and second caliphs of Islam. Abu Bakr (caliph from 632 to 634) was one of Islam's first adepts and the father of Aïcha, one of Mohammed's wives. Omar (caliph from 634 to 644) was the father of Hafça, another of Mohammed's wives (*Encyclopaedia of Islam*, I, pp. 80-82; III, pp. 982-4; Gaudefroy-Demombynes, pp. 79, 129).

19
Anonymous
Koran Commentary, no date
32 x 48 cm (12.5 x 19 in)
Royal Museum of Central Africa, Tervuren

A reading of the Koran given by Fatima, the daughter of Mohammed and the wife of Ali.

20
Anonymous
Prayer on the Waves, no date
33 x 42 cm (13 x 16.5 in)
Private collection

The miracle of the prayer on the waves has been attributed to several famous saints of Islam and revived to the advantage of Sheikh Amadu Bamba, founder of the Mouride brotherhood (see pl. 30). Here, however, the saint is most likely an Algerian one (Strobel, p. 51).

21

Anonymous
Prayer on the Waves, no date
24 x 23 cm (9.5 x 9 in)
Royal Museum of Central Africa, Tervuren

Again, the subject is the miracle of the prayer on the waves, this time with a Moorish sheikh (Strobel, p. 52).

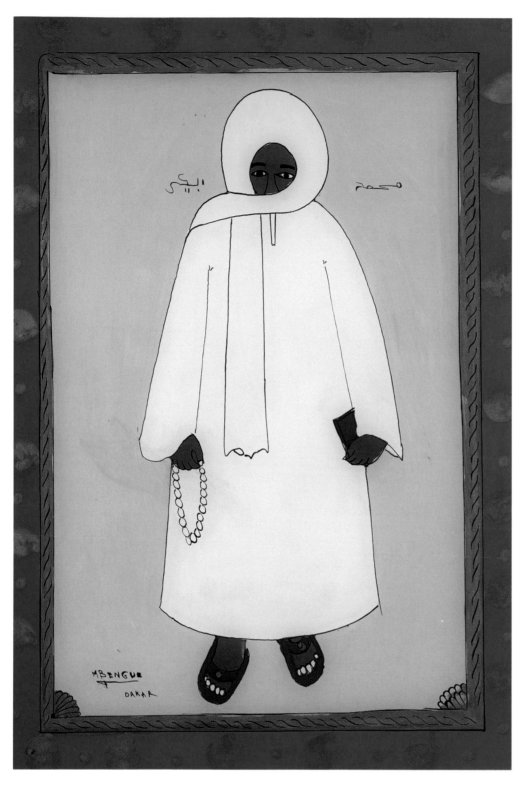

22

Gora Mbengue
Sheikh Amadu Bamba, no date
48 x 33 cm (19 x 13 in)
Private collection

Based on the only known photograph of Sheikh Amadu Bamba, which was taken in 1913, this painting shows him standing, dressed entirely in white, his face half-hidden by a scarf.

23

Gora Mbengue
The Submission of Ibra Fall, 1983
33 x 48 cm (13 x 19 in)
Private collection

Sheikh Ibra Fall, the first disciple of Amadu
Bamba, was a former *ceddo*, that is, a cap-
tive warrior close to the Wolof kings. The
scene here shows Ibra Fall in submission before Amadu Bamba, implicitly renouncing
his former pagan life. He became very ac-
tive in spreading his master's word, bringing to him many disciples. He was also
the initiator, through his own earnest efforts
in agricultural labour, of the policies that
turned the Mouride brotherhood into a
major regional economic power–the peanut
lobby! The central minaret of the mosque at
Touba is called *lamp*, a reference to Ibra
Fall's nickname (Cruise O'Brien, pp. 141-8).

24

Anonymous
Wandering of the Marabout, no date
30 x 48 cm (12 x 19 in)
Private collection

Amadu Bamba is travelling on horseback in
search of a site for his mosque, finally built
at Touba (Strobel, pp. 107-8). The white feet
and face his horse displays symbolize the
five pillars of Islam (Boisdur, p. 104). The
person who is supposed to have accompanied Amadu Bamba at this time was Ibra
Fall, who is always represented with black
hair. According to Babacar Lo, the old man
with a white beard and hair that we see
here is Sheikh Ibrahim Mbake, one of
Amadu Bamba's brothers. He carries the *satala* (ablution vessel) containing the water
one uses for the ritual ablutions that pre-
cede prayer. In Senegal the *satala* is also
used for personal washing. It is mandatory
to use the left hand (which is considered im-
pure) when washing, and only the right one
when eating from the common plate. Any di-
vergence from this custom during a meal
would result in the immediate departure of
any guests present, for it would be seen by
them as a grave insult.

The Mourides brotherhood   59

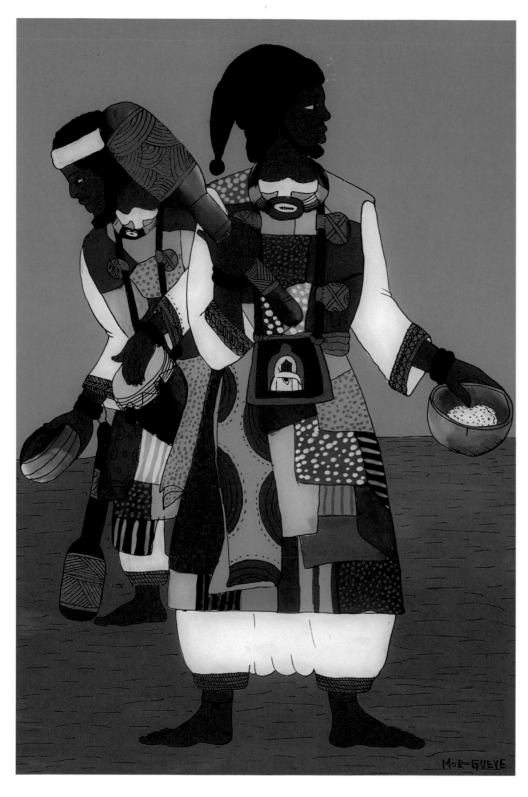

25

Mor Gueye

Bay Fall, no date

48 x 33 cm (19 x 13 in)

Private collection

The Bay Fall, so called in memory of their
master, Sheikh Ibra Fall (see pl. 23), the
first disciple of Sheikh Amadu Bamba, com-
prise a particular group within the Mouride
brotherhood, for, as 'policemen' and beg-
gars, they have a joint role. During the
Touba Magal (the annual pilgrimage of the
Mourides) they 'regulate the traffic' and control the movements of the crowd thronging
before the mosque. They also wander the
streets shaking their bowls and collecting
money. On occasion they scourge themselves ritually, using the *xiir*, a bludgeon,
also a symbol of fecundity, one of their
attributes. They can be recognized by their
long hair (*sëxe bopp*) gathered in locks –
similar to those of the Jamaican 'rasta
men' – and by their *caaya* (wide trousers
with the crotch at ankle level) made of
patched pieces of cloth in bright colours.
They often wear a black woollen cap and
numerous amulets (Strobel, pp. 99-101).
They are deemed a heretical group of the
brotherhood by more orthodox Mourides
because of their exemption from prayer and
fasting, compensations for their assiduous
agricultural work (Cruise O'Brien,
pp. 141-58; Monteil, 1966(a), pp. 185-6).

26

Arona Diarra

The Arrest of Sheikh Amadu Bamba,
no date

32 x 48 cm (12.5 x 19 in)
Private collection

This painting very likely represents the time when Amadu Bamba, still accompanied by Ibra Fall, was taken into custody by the French before his imprisonment in Dakar and his subsequent exile in Gabon. It is also possible that this scene simply recalls another episode in Bamba's life when he met the French and no confrontation took place.

27

Gora Mbengue (unsigned)
Amadu Bamba and the Lion, no date
33 x 48 cm (13 x 19 in)
Private collection

Bamba's imprisonment in Dakar generated several legendary tales in which he, with help from God, faced the ordeals to which he was subjected by the French authorities. In one a famished lion was locked in the same cell as Bamba, but instead of devouring him, the lion quietly lay down by his side (Boisdur, p. 110).

28

Gora Mbengue
Amadu Bamba and the Bull, 1984
33 x 48 cm (13 x 19 in)
Private collection

Another of Amadu Bamba's miraculous adventures. Here, in an arena, he is confronted by a bull, which, instead of goring him, drops dead at his feet (Boisdur, p. 110).

29
Mor Gueye
Amadu Bamba's Imprisonment in Dakar, 1993
33 x 48 cm (13 x 19 in)
Royal Museum of Central Africa, Tervuren

In this episode the Touba *sëriñ* is shown emerging unharmed from the spike-studded cell in which he had been locked.

30

Anonymous

Prayer on the Waves, no date

33 x 40 cm (13 x 16 in)
Private collection

This is one of the most famous episodes in Amadu Bamba's life. The captain of the ship taking Bamba into exile in Gabon provokes him by forbidding him to pray, arguing that 'If you pray on my ship, you offend me; if you do not pray, you offend your God'. To avoid offending either, the *marabout* is said to have unrolled his prayer mat on the waves. Here, we can definitely see the influence of earlier reverse-glass paintings, and no doubt the 'prayer on the waves' of Arab or Maghrebi saints (pls. 20 and 21) were inspired by the story of Christ walking on the water. The Mouride ideology thus incorporates striking events or details that impress the imagination, crystallize faith and generate veneration of a saint. Even the flying angels in this painting remind us of those who came to rescue Mohammed during the Battle of Badr (pl. 13). What could be more miraculous and inspiring than the legend of a man who responded to intolerant enemies without violence, but chose instead to pray to his God in complete serenity among the blessed fish. Aboard the ship are three allegorical figures, all disproportionally large, that represent a foreign and oppressive culture: the white woman (a defiled temptress), the missionary (Christian meddlings in African affairs on African territory), and the uniformed captain (the colonial administration, with its brutal resort to force). By persecuting him, the French made a martyr of Amadu Bamba; the result was that the colonial power unintentionally served as a propaganda tool for Islam.

31

Babacar Lo (Lô Ba)
Sheikh Amadu Bamba and the 'jinn',
1994
33 x 48 cm (13 x 19 in)
Royal Museum of Central Africa, Tervuren

Another episode in Sheikh Amadu Bamba's exile in Gabon. Here we see him, imperturbable on his prayer mat, confronted with terrifying visions of evil monsters and *jinn* (genies and spirits, *jinne* in Wolof), assisted during this ordeal by Jibril (Gabriel), the good angel or genie *par excellence*. At his side, prey to anguish and despair, is Samba Laobe Penda, the former king of Jolof, who was exiled at the same time as Bamba (Cruise O'Brien, p. 42), and who seems to want both to protect his companion and seek refuge behind him. All Bamba's attributes are gathered nearby: sandals, chaplet, book, case and *satala*. Curiously, this epi-sode recalls Ali's fight against Ras Al-Ghoul, the monstrous Yemenite prince, half-man, half-beast, with Ali the civilizing hero through whom a new order is established (Aziza, p. 60; Strobel, pp. 113-18). For Amadu Bamba, this period of exile was an opportunity for contemplation, meditation and prayer; he himself wrote that he 'conducted a holy war against his passions' Monteil, 1996(a), p. 165), the expression of which we see here in symbolic form.

33

Babacar Lo (Lô Ba)
The Sacrifice at Darou Salam, 1994
33 x 48 cm (13 x 19 in)
Royal Museum of Central Africa, Tervuren

On his return to Senegal in 1902, Sheikh Amadu Bamba first settled in Darou Salam (Cruise O'Brien, p. 44), where he asked for one animal of each species to be sacrificed. One man volunteered himself too, but Bamba refused this gesture of extreme devotion. Some versions have it that Amadu's brother-in-law suggested that a child be sacrificed as well, though we see nothing of that here (Boisdur, p. 114).

32

Anonymous
The Massacre of the French, no date
37 x 48 cm (15 x 19 in)
Royal Museum of Central Africa, Tervuren

The setting appears to be in Gabon, for it is probably Samba Laobe Penda (see pl. 31) whom we see again at the side of Sheikh Amadu Bamba, here humbly holding his master's *satala*. The violent scene records a mutiny among the French troops, who are slaughtering one another while a host of angels intervenes on Bamba's behalf: while one angel sets fire to Bamba's cell, another seems to be exhorting a soldier to destroy his compatriot; a 'battle of Badr' in the twentieth century that serves to advance the cause of the Mouride Sheikh. As in the prayer on the waves (pl. 30) we have, in the foreground, the figures of the officer and the white woman, symbols of degenerate colonial power; here they gaze on the disaster that colonial injustice has brought down on its own agents. Once again, too, the figure of Bamba is made disproportionately large, for in the art of reverse-glass painting the size of a figure is intimately linked to the degree of importance the person it represents actually has, or to the ideological meaning he or she conveys. To claim that this form of perspective – in which meaning transmitted by relative size takes precedence over a scientifically organized ocular coherence – proves that reverse-glass painting is crude and naive, is woefully to misunderstand the nature and meaning of the tradition in which Senegalese artists continue to work. On the contrary, we are confronted with an art-form that reveals no superfluous details, only strong, striking images representing concepts sacred to any Mouride Moslem. In the end, despite his intolerance, William Ponty most likely judged these images with more discernment than some of our contemporaries!

34
Anonymous
Masamba Mbake, no date
24 x 18 cm (9.5 x 7 in)
Private collection

A formal portrait of one of Sheikh Amadu Bamba's brothers.

35

Babacar Lo (Mbaye Lo)
El Hadj Malick Sy and his Sons, 1952
40 x 50 cm (16 x 20 in)
Private collection

Painted in 1952 by Babacar Lo, who at that time signed his works 'Mbaye Lo', this work is one of his earliest examples that is both signed and dated. The slightly upturned staring eyes, with their pronounced whites, is characteristic of Babacar Lo's portraits of this period. In the centre is El Hadj Malick

Sy, easily identifiable by his umbrella, here surrounded by four of his sons: top right is Ababacar Sy (the second son), top left is El Hadj Mansur Sy (the third), bottom right is El Hadj Abdu Aziz Sy (the fourth), currently caliph of Dakar, and bottom left is Abibu Sy (the fifth). Note that, under the influence of the way that written Arabic is transmitted, these formal images are arranged in a chronological progression from right to left. The first son, Mustapha Sy, is not shown here, for he died in France during the First World War (information from Babacar Lo, Decem-

ber 1993); Abdu Aziz Sy is, in fact, the only one alive today. The umbrella-wielding El Hadj Malick Sy was succeeded by Ababacar Sy, who was the first caliph of the Tijaan until his death on 25 March 1957; El Hadj Mansur Sy, the next in line, unfortunately died only four days later, thus El Hadj Abdu Aziz Sy, after some conflict and rivalry within the family, took over (Samb, 1972, p. 333).

36

Anonymous

Ahmed Tijani at Prayer, no date

40 x 50 cm (16 x 20 in)

Private collection

It is said that during a prayer at the mosque a snake threatened to disturb the service led by Ahmed Tijani, who without pausing, seized and mastered the creature (Strobel, pp. 158-9).

37

Anonymous
El Hadj Malick Sy, no date
45 x 37 cm (17.5 x 15 in)
Royal Museum of Central Africa, Tervuren

Inspired by a photograph of El Hadj Malick Sy taken in front of the mosque at Tiva- ouane, this painting shows him sheltered under an umbrella and wearing the gar- ment of those who made the pilgrimage to Mecca.

38

Anonymous
El Hadj Malick Sy, no date
50 x 40 cm (20 x 16 in)
Private collection

Based on the same photograph as the one that inspired plate 37, here the image has been reversed, so that El Hadj Malick Sy appears holding his umbrella in his right hand. Reversals of this sort are not uncom- mon: we know, for instance, that in some cases the illustrations in Renaudeau and Strobel's book have been used as models for drawings, which were then reversed for images that form the basic image in reverse-glass paintings.

39
Anonymous
Ababacar Sy, no date
48 x 36 cm (19 x 14 in)
Private collection

Here the first caliph of the Tijaan, El Hadj
Malick Sy's successor, is shown with his
French military medals pinned to his chest.
With him is a Tabaski sheep, decorated with
amulets, a reminder of Abraham's sacrifice
(see pl. 8).

40
Anonymous
Ababacar Sy, no date
47 x 38 cm (18.5 x 15 in)
Royal Museum of Central Africa, Tervuren

As in plate 39, Ababacar Sy is recorded
proudly wearing his French medals and
decorations.

41
Anonymous
El Hadj Malick Sy and his Sons, no date
40 x 50 cm (16 x 20 in)
Royal Museum of Central Africa, Tervuren

In the centre is El Hadj Malick Sy; from right to left appear Ababacar Sy, El Hadj Mansur Sy, El Hadj Abdu Aziz Sy and Abibu Sy.

42

Anonymous
Mandione Laye, no date
48 x 38 cm (19 x 15 in)
Private collection

The second caliph of the Layen brotherhood is shown here with the 'ethereal phaeton' sea-bird, also called the 'red-billed Tro-
pic bird', on his shoulder. On his brother's
death in 1949, Mandione Laye took over the
leadership of the brotherhood. It is said
that, in 1950, when he presided over the
first Korité prayer, which ends the fasting
period of Ramadan, one of these birds flew
down and settled on his shoulder. Ever
since, the bird has remained the emblem of
the brotherhood, and the black and white
turban of the *marabouts* is a reminder of its
plumage. There is a famous photograph of
Mandione Laye where we see him posing,
with an 'ethereal phaeton' on his knee
(Sylla, p. 639); many reverse-glass paintings
have revived this image.

43

Anonymous
Ethereal Phaeton, no date
38 x 48 cm (15 x 19 in)
Private collection

The 'ethereal phaeton' represented alone
is a straightforward symbol of the Layen
brotherhood.

44

Anonymous

Issa Rohu Laye, no date

38 x 30 cm (15 x 12 in)

Royal Museum of Central Africa, Tervuren

A portrait of the first caliph of the Layen brotherhood, son of the founder, Limamu Laye. The flower of the prickly pear that we see at his side perhaps conveys an esoteric message, as this brotherhood seems to have cultivated a taste for obscure imagery. The ring (found in the sea) that Issa Laye displays on his finger is supposedly that of Solomon, and gives him power over the *jinn* (Strobel, p. 149).

76   Islam and Senegalese brotherhoods

45

Anonymous

Sheikh Sidiya Baba, Abd El Qadir El Jilani and Sheikh Amadu Bamba

32 x 48 cm (13 x 19 in)

Royal Museum of Central Africa, Tervuren

Sheikh Sidiya Baba, Amadu Bamba's Mauritanian Qadir master, is shown at the side of the brotherhood's founder, Abd El Qadir El Jilani. The figure of Sheikh Amadu Bamba completes the link regarding this brotherhood, for with him, and founded on Qadir teaching, a new brotherhood was brought into being – the Mourides brotherhood.

46

Gora Mbengue

The Marabouts, no date

21 x 50 cm (8 x 20 in)

Royal Museum of Central Africa, Tervuren

These various *marabouts* belong to the four great Senegalese brotherhoods. From left to right: Sheikh Tienaba Seck (Tijaan), El Hadj Malick Sy (Tijaan), Masamba Mbake (Mouride), Limamu Laye (Layen), Sheikh Sa Hadji Bu Qadir (Qadir), Sheikh Amadu Bamba (Mouride) and Ibrahima Niasse (Tijaan).

47

Anonymous

Abd El Qadir El Jilani, no date

60 x 46 cm (23.5 x 18 in)

Private collection

A portrait of the Arab founder of the Qadir brotherhood.

48

Gora Mbengue
'Lat Dior N'Gonné Lattir', 1985
33 x 48 cm (13 x 19 in)
Private collection

Lat Dior, the *damel* (king) of Cayor stands by the side of his black horse, recognizable by the white spots on its legs and face. Lat Dior himself can be identified by his red cape, cap and boots. The stump to the left is probably a baobab tree, wreathed in amulets.

49

Ibrahima Sall
Lat Dior and Demba War Sal, no date
33 x 48 cm (13 x 19 in)
Private collection

In this painting we can easily recognize Lat Dior's horse and his own red cap. He is accompanied by his faithful adviser, Demba War Sal, chief of the crown's captives, many of whom served the King as *ceddo* (warriors). Indeed, Wolof society in Lat Dior's day was stratified by caste, and a great deal of its cohesion depended on these slaves of the state, some of whom held very high positions. It is said that Lat Dior owed his fall to the conflicts with Demba War. In 1886, the year of his death, Cayor lost its status as a kingdom and became a confederation of six provinces presided over by Demba War Sal (Monteil, 1966 (a), pp. 85-8, 91-3).

78   Profane genres and themes

50
Babacar Lo (Lô Ba)
Lat Dior, 1994
33 x 48 cm (13 x 19 in)
Royal Museum of Central Africa, Tervuren

Lat Dior, with his usual attributes. Only the cap is special, for otherwise this image conforms to those stereotypical ones. Lat Dior Ngonê Latir Diop (his full name) was born *c.* 1842. Born into an animistic society, he attended a Koranic school, though his conversion to Islam did not take place until 1864.

Because of internal squabbling he did not accede directly to the throne of Cayor, and for a while it was held by one Makodu, until the French expelled him in 1861 and installed Madiodio in his place. The following year, however, Lat Dior regained his throne and was made *damel*, or king. He lost it three years later and was forced to leave for Sine Saloum, where he stayed for four years. He then returned to Cayor, but had to wait until 1871 to be recognized as *damel* by the French. His relations remained fairly good with the colonial administration until

1882, the year he opposed the construction of a railway between Dakar and St-Louis. Made destitute once more, he withdrew to Baol. On 26 October 1886 he was killed during the Battle of Deqele (Monteil, 1966 (a), pp. 90-101). The sole Wolof sovereign to have converted to Islam (Diop, p. 234), and at the end of his life a fierce opponent of French colonization, Lat Dior is an apt symbol of the flux in nineteenth-century Senegalese culture, a society constrained by numerous binding traditions but one that was also in search of new paths to follow.

51

Anonymous

Lat Dior (?), no date

24 x 30 cm (9.5 x 12 in)

Private collection

The horse in this painting seems to be that of the *damel* of Cayor, but the rider's outfit does not conform at all to what one might expect Lat Dior to be wearing – red cape, cap and boots. Indeed, Alburi Ndiaye is the ruler one so often encounters dressed in white (Boisdur, p. 125). So this equestrian portrait may well be one of this other sovereign (*buur-ba*) of Jolof (1842-1900), who was also famous for his courageous opposition to the invading French (Ndiaye Leyti, pp. 993-4).

52

Gora Mbengue
Kocc Barma, 1985
33 x 48 cm (13 x 19 in)
Royal Museum of Central Africa, Tervuren

Kocc Barma is here presented in the same stereotypical manner as the great national heroes of Senegal, although this particular celebrity, a colourful seventeenth-century philosopher, became famous through an unusual form of resistance against an oppressor, in this case the King, Dauda Demba (Searing, p. 17). The legend has it that Kocc Barma displayed four tufts of hair on his otherwise shaved scalp, the meaning of which escaped everyone. The King demanded to know more and had him arrested. Kocc refused to give the slightest ex-planation, and was thus imprisoned. His wife, however, following the promises of wealth made to her by the King, did not hesitate for long before betraying her husband and re-vealing the hidden meaning of the locks. They were related symbolically to four sayings: *buur du mbokk* (the King is not a relative); *jigeen sopal, te bul woolu* (love your wife but do not trust her); *doom u jiitle du doom, ay la* (the adopted child is not a son but a source of problems); and *maget mat na baay ci reew* (the old also deserve a place in the community). Kocc persisted in his refusal to speak and the King decided to execute him, but before the sentence was carried out, Kocc's adopted son ran to take back the blanket his 'father' had on his back, to avoid blood being spilt on it. Then an old man intervened to suggest clemency to the King, putting forward the fact that the punishment would not give him the key to the puzzle. At this moment Kocc Barma agreed to reveal the sayings to which his four locks referred, since he could, by the same token, prove their veracity. Thus the King is no relative, for despite having spent their childhood together, he does not take into account his links with Kocc Barma and is ready to kill him; the problems he, Kocc Barma, is facing are the result of a lack of discretion on the part of his wife; his adopted son is nobody's son since he shows himself ready to strip his father at the moment of execution; and, finally, it is due to the intervention of an old man that he is still alive (Monteil, 1966 (a), p. 80).

LE CHASSEUR D'ESCLAVE

53

Gora Mbengue
The Slave Hunter, 1985
32 x 48 cm (13 x 19 in)
Private collection

The *ceddo*, the traditional Wolof warrior, often hunted slaves with a lasso, as if they were animals. In the Wolof kingdoms, most *ceddos* were actually slaves themselves, the *jaam u buur* (the slaves of the Crown). One cannot but be moved by the absurdity and cruelty involved in the seizure of blacks to be made slaves by their African brothers. Here, as we see, slaves chase fellow blacks in order to sell them, exile them, deprive them of their status as human beings.

54
Gora Mbengue
Slave, 1985
48 x 32 cm (19 x 13 in)
Private collection

A scourged slave. This vision of a slave
and his torturer is all the more poignant
because of the free rein it gives to the imagination: our own minds invent the face dis-
torted by the pain of the one, and the face
of the other also, satiated with sadistic pleasure. Yet Gora Mbengue merely shows us
their backs: the victim's receiving the
blows, the tormentor's full of an extraordinary violence. The latter's expands in one
mighty effort, channelling all his energy
into the arm about to strike, with his spread
legs giving him the stability of a rock. Here
Gora Mbengue manipulates our emotions
with a drawing reduced to its simplest com-
ponents: a few lines of force – sober, accu-
rate, ineluctable.

55
Gora Mbengue
Slaves in Gaol, 1985
32 x 48 cm (12.5 x 19 in)
Private collection

56

Gora Mbengue
Crocodiles Waiting for Slaves, no date
32 x 48 cm (12.5 x 19 in)
Private collection

A group of trussed slaves is being carried
off in a boat. All are in tears. On the right,
an old man implores God for mercy. A
mother who, powerless, sees her child fed
to the crocodiles, can do nothing but hide
her face.

57
Mor Gueye
Arms and the Slave Trade, 1990
33 x 48 cm (13 x 19 in)
Private collection

A pair of white traders have arrived in a village, whereupon they offer arms in exchange for human merchandise.

58

Mor Gueye
The House of Slaves at Gorée,
1992
33 x 48 cm (13 x 19 in)
Private collection

A black and white composition, both in
theme and tone. The white officer in his uni-
form, conceited and haughty, dominates the
scene by his height as well as by his posi-
tion in the organization of the image. The
black slaves are crushed, small, crumpled
and separated, with the women on one side
and the men on the other, just as the house
of slaves was actually arranged. At the 'door
of no return', a gaping black hole, is a slave
squatting in front of the inescapable fate
that awaits him. There are a few contemporary 'scholarly' artists who work in black
and white, but Mor Gueye is the only traditional one who does so.

59
Gora Mbengue
Punished Slave, 1985
48 x 32 cm (19 x 13 in)
Private collection

Against a blood-red background is a slave
bound with emphasis on (golden) chains,
handcuffs and muzzle. Even the tree appears minuscule next to this man, para-
lysed with suffering.

60

Moussa Lo
Sabar, no date
24 x 32 cm (9.5 x 12.5 cm)
Private collection

The *sabar*, a well-known Wolof dance, demands a lot of skill and speed. It is constructed on a series of notes played against the beat in very complex rhythms imposed by the percussionist. The development of the *sabar* rests on a dialogue between the soloist and the dancer. The rhythm is at first given by a group of drummers (at least three); each has an instrument struck by means of a stick and with the flat of the hand. At this warming-up stage, the rhythm settles in, vigorous but steady. The specta-

tors form a circle and clap their hands. One of them, usually a woman, moves forward into the middle of the circle, facing the musicians. At this moment, the percussion soloist often leaves the group to meet the dancer, as we see in this picture. Next comes a stage of extremely rapid dialogue: the other musicians maintain and accelerate the basic rhythm while the soloist inspires the dancer to move, imposing on her unexpected stops and lashing re-entries. As for the dancer, she responds to the given rhythms but also directs or encourages musical phrases. We thus witness performances in which neither the dancer nor the musician any longer knows who is in charge. The smallest feast is a pretext to organize a *sabar*, especially baptisms and weddings.

It is a dance that can sometimes appear licentious because it generates very sensual movements, but above all it is a game of seduction, not a prelude to debauchery. In the 1970s President Senghor attempted in vain to ban its more extravagant forms, thinking that it might shock ill-informed visitors. Indeed, some old texts referring to the *sabar* describe it as devilish, unbridled, a mimic of copulation, and other prejudicial commonplaces (Le Cour Grandmaison, pp. 139-40). Anyone who has ever tried to learn this dance knows that it demands endurance, perseverance, assiduous limbering-up and, above all, training in one of the most elaborate of all African rhythms.

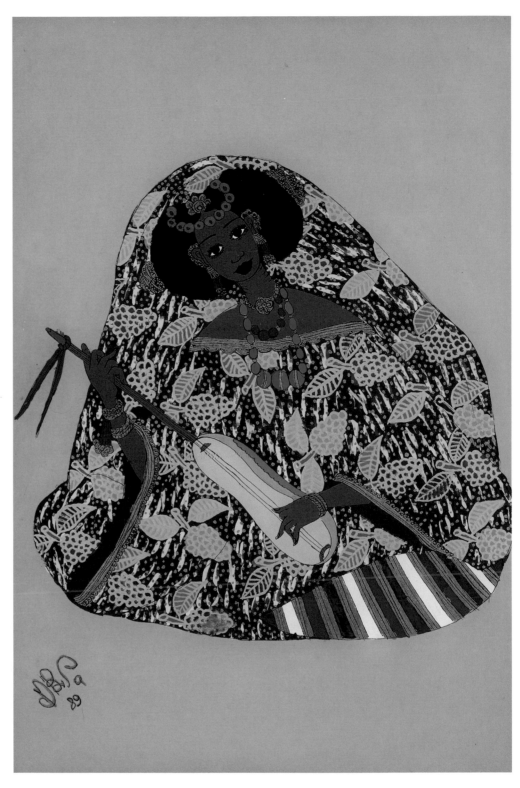

61
Mbida
Xalam-player, 1989
48 x 33 cm (19 x 13 in)
Royal Museum of Central Africa, Tervuren

The *xalam* is a three-string guitar.

63
Paco
Sabar Dancer, no date
33 x 25 cm (13 x 10 in)
Private collection

64

Mbida

Musicians, no date

33 x 48 cm (13 x 19 in)

Private collection

A group of five musicians, in the centre of whom is the *balafon* player. The *balafon* is a xylophone made up of wooden blades resting on a wooden structure. Sheltered by this structure, calabashes of various sizes form the sound-boxes. To the left, we have the *kora*-player, whose instrument is related to the harp family. The *kora* is a big calabash (sound-box) surmounted by a stave on which 24 strings are arranged. Next is a musician with a *xalam*, a three-string guitar (see pl. 61), one with a *ritiy*, a small three-string harp played with a bow, and finally, to the right, a flute-player (see pl. 62).

65
Mbida
A Kora-player, 1992
32 x 24 cm (12.5 x 9.5 in)
Private collection

The inspirer of this picture is Mahawa Kouyate, a famous Senegalese singer. Mbida particularly likes the instrument she holds, the
kora. One of the greatest *kora*-players is
Sundiulu Cissoko, Mahawa Kouyate's husband, but he has too hoarse a voice for
Mbida's taste. Since in this painting Mbida
wanted to celebrate his delight in the sound
of the *kora* and Mahawa's voice, he chose
to unite the individual talents of each in a
portrait of Mahawa Kouyate holding the
instrument.

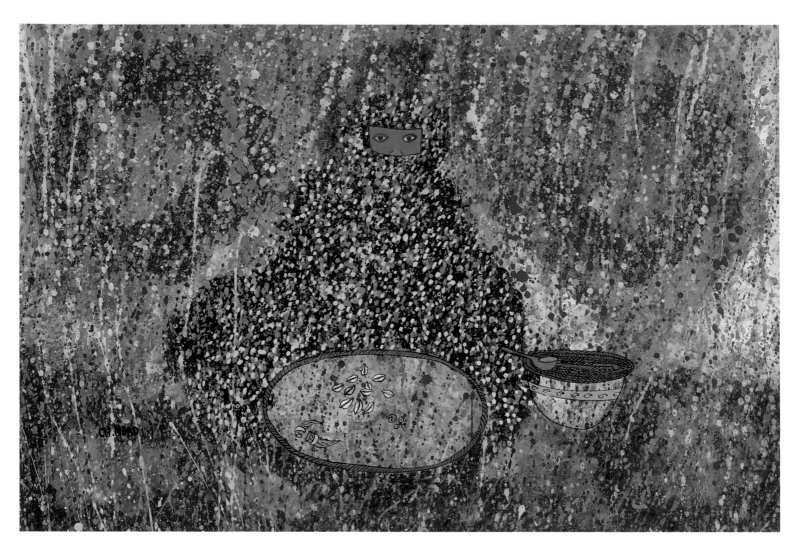

66
Cheikh Ndao
Divination, no date
33 x 48 cm (13 x 19 in)
Private collection

Treated in an abstract way, this is a divination (see pl. 93) carried out by a woman. Somewhere between dream and fantasy, a mysterious character wearing a deep-blue face plays with the cowries of fate.

67
Cheikh Ndao
Dancer, no date
33 x 24 cm (13 x 9.5 in)
Private collection

Lost in the complexity and the speed of her steps, this figure of a dancer emerges from a blue magma or, perhaps, melts into it. The rhythm alone is insisted on by means of the two percussion instruments precisely delineated in the foreground. The three flaps we see on each drum are metallic plates whose periphery is garnished with iron rings; these vibrate sympathetically to the rhythm.

68

Babacar Lo (Lô Ba)
Wedding-day, 1993
33 x 48 cm (13 x 19 in)
Private collection

In Senegalese society, on her wedding day the woman leaves her own parents to join those of her husband. We see here a woman, face hidden, on horseback, preceded by the *marabout* and the *griots*, and followed by two females who carry her dishes and other goods. It is thought proper that a woman should appear very tearful on her wedding day, since she abandons the parental home to live with a new family.

69
Babacar Lo (Lô Ba)
The Eloped Bride, 1993
48 x 33 cm (19 x 13 in)
Private collection

Weddings by abduction most often result
from a plan in which two young people in
love elope together in order to force their
respective families to accept their union.

70
Ibrahima Sall
Market, no date
32 x 48 cm (12.5 x 19 in)
Royal Museum of Central
Africa, Tervuren

71
Moussa Johnson
Market, 1993
24 x 33 cm (9.5 x 13 in)
Royal Museum of Central
Africa, Tervuren

72

Mbida
Kermel Market, Dakar, 1992
33 x 48 cm (13 x 19 in)
Private collection

This market, chiefly visited by tourists, included a covered area, whose structures we see in the background. In 1993 a fire completely destroyed the building, and the merchants who had worked indoors (notably those who were selling reverse-glass paintings) were forced to set up their stalls in the streets across from the marketplace.

73
Gabou
Car-rapide, 1994
33 x 48 cm (13 x 19 in)
Private collection

The *car-rapide*, or express-coach, is the most popular means of public transportation in Dakar. Unlike the buses, it is used solely to connect suburbs to town centres. The driver has an assistant who remains on the back footplate of the vehicle and warns him when one of the passengers wants to get off by hitting a window with a handful of coins. It is the assistant who collects the fares and shouts out the destinations. The stops are more or less fixed, but in many cases it is established usage rather than formal signs that designates them as such. Be-

fore a driver sets off he waits until he has a full coach, and so the passengers just clamber aboard and wait. At rush hour, however, when people leave Dakar to go back home to the suburbs or beyond, one regularly witnesses scenes similar to that reproduced here: people throng, fight for a seat on the first coach, and do not hesitate to climb in through the windows. The *cars-rapides* are painted in blue and yellow, and they are also often decorated with various patterns and inscriptions, for which teams of painters are responsible. On this particular *car-rapide* we read '*Al khamdouli lahi*', an expression invoking Allah's name; '*Senegal suma reew*' (Senegal, my country); '*nanga deef*' (How do you do?); and, on the front, a list of destinations: Sandaga (the big market in the centre of Dakar), and two suburbs,

Pikine and Grand Yoff. Frequently, one also encounters inscriptions that relate to the driver's brotherhood or warn of his great temerity. Among the people in this painting we see a hawker, a handicapped person begging, a man losing his horse-race betting slips (a sport to which many Senegalese are passionately dedicated) and a character dear to Gabou, a man who always takes advantage of such situations by putting his hand on the backside of the nearest available woman! And note too the amusing detail of the European, already well-trained in Dakar habits, clambering in through the back window.

74
Gabou
Taxi-brousse, 1994
33 x 48 cm (13 x 19 in)
Private collection

The bush-taxi connects town with town. It leaves from a coach station, but only once the driver decides enough passengers are on board. There are several kinds of bush-taxi, and the fare charged relates to the number of persons each can carry. Even so, they are inevitably loaded to their maximum capacity, and the luggage-rack always carries more than one can imagine it is capable of. This vehicle has a portrait of Sheikh Amadu Bamba on the side, and an inscription '*borom Touba*' (the master of Touba). Once again, the scene is rich with drama: a woman, the victim of the driver's abruptness, has dropped her calabash packed with all the necessary ingredients for the daily *ceebu jën* (rice with fish). Her loin-cloth, caught under the nearside rear wheel, is coming undone, to the delight of the passengers, including the usual rascal of Gabou's paintings, who has almost dropped his prayer chaplet. This small roadside incident reveals to us the *jel jelli*: inner belts of beads that women wear around the hips, seductive objects whose rows knock against one another during dances.

75
Arona Diarra
Departure for the Touba Magal, no date
33 × 48 cm (13 × 19 in)
Private collection

The Touba Magal is the pilgrimage of the Mourides, organized every year to commem-orate Sheikh Amadu Bamba's return from exile in 1902. From every region of Senegal, cars, coaches and trucks – overloaded with fervent Mourides, tourists and onlookers – flock to Touba. Special trains are assigned to transport the crowds heading for the holy place, and all available space is monopol-ized in order to receive the pilgrims – cattle trucks, car roofs, etc. Conditions during the journey are dreadful: countless people faint, some collapse; road and rail accidents are frequent. However, every Mouride is keen to participate in this pilgrimage, which of-ten involves enormous sacrifices (Samb, 1969, pp. 736-44). In the foreground, to the left, is a Bay Fall (see pl. 25).

76
Ibrahima Sall
Ferry-boat
33 x 48 cm (13 x 19 in)
Private collection

Crossing the River Gambia en route for Casamance.

77
Mbida
Fisherman, no date
32 x 48 cm (12.5 x 19 in)
Private collection

78
Jules
On a Bike, no date
24 × 33 cm (9.5 × 13 in)
Royal Museum of Central Africa, Tervuren

79
Arona Diarra
On a Bike, no date
24 × 33 cm (9.5 × 13 in)
Royal Museum of Central Africa, Tervuren

80
Moussa Johnson
Going to the Goat Market, 1993
24 x 30 cm (9.5 x 12 in)
Royal Museum of Central Africa, Tervuren

81
Gora Mbengue
The Photographer, 1982
33 x 48 cm (13 x 19 in)
Private collection

A painting made for the Michel Renaudeau photographic studio in Dakar. (Michel Renaudeau is co-author, with M. Strobel, of a book dedicated to reverse-glass painting in Senegal; see the Bibliography.)

82
Mor Gueye
The Opthalmologist, 1992
24 x 33 cm (9.5 x 13 in)
Private collection

83
Babacar Lo (Lô Ba)
At the Tailor's Shop, 1993
48 x 33 cm (19 x 13 in)
Private collection

84

Gora Mbengue
The Hunters, no date
32 x 48 cm (12.5 x 19 in)
Private collection

More than just a scene of everyday life, this painting is a warning to imprudent hunters. The image could be included in the section in this book dedicated to Wolof tales and proverbs, for it recalls two sayings: *boo xamoon li lay yoot, nga bayyi li ngay yoot* (If you knew what was on the lookout for you, you would drop what you are looking out for), and *lu waye def, sa bopp* (literally, What you do is your head, or in other words, One harvests the consequences of one's acts) (Ndiaye, K., pp. 40-41).

85

Ibrahima Sall
Wrestlers, no date
33 x 48 cm (13 x 19 in)
Private collection

Wrestling, a popular sport in Senegal, is practised every weekend in the stadia at Dakar. The spectacle lies not solely in the actual confrontations, for there are various entertainments to enjoy too, notably the entrance dance of the wrestlers, who are decorated with *gris-gris* (protective amulets). The sole goal in wrestling is to force one's opponent to the ground. This painting depicts two famous combatants, Diéri Sadio and Madoune Khoulé; here they are poised to begin grappling with one another. The drum symbolizes the rhythm and dance that are essential aspects of this sport.

86
Azu Bade
Cooking, 1994
33 x 48 cm (13 x 19 in)
Private collection

87
Mor Gueye
Two Farmers, 1993
24 x 33 cm (9.5 x 13 in)
Private collection

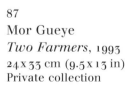

These could very well be Diola or Manjaku farmers (people from the south-west of Senegal or from Guinea-Bissau), for the agricultural instrument the man carries is what the Diola call *kajendo* and the Manjaku *bërëpët*. This is the tool that is used for ploughing the fields.

88

Gora Mbengue

Casamance, 1984

32 x 48 cm (12.5 x 19 in)

Private collection

An idyllic vision of Casamance, the southern region known as the granary of Senegal because of its abundant cultivation. Nearby live the Diola, chiefly rice cultivators, some of whom are currently struggling for the secession of the region. One of their villages is represented here. There are houses, with impluvia, whose architecture is famous in Africa, and in the left foreground are a split drum and the two mallets. The village gives the impression of having fallen asleep, the time of day when the siesta is taken.

89
Mbida
Koranic School, 1992
33 x 48 cm (13 x 19 in)
Private collection

A *marabout* in front of his *taalibe* (disciples,
or pupils), who are equipped with the small
boards on which verses of the Koran are
written.

90
Khaly
The Marabout's Meal, no date
29 x 40 cm (11 x 16 in)
Royal Museum of Central Africa, Tervuren

This *marabout* is enjoying a good feast, while the little *taalibe* entrusted to him are watching on the sly.

91
Khaly
The Sleeping Taalibe, no date
33 x 43 cm (13 x 17 in)
Private collection

The strict *marabout*, equipped with his *satala* (ablution vessel), runs his eye over the wretched room in which his *taalibe* are crammed. As in plate 90, this painting belongs to the series that Khaly dedicated to the children entrusted to unscrupulous *marabouts*.

92
Arona Diarra
Wure-players, no date
24 x 33 cm (9.5 x 13 in)
Private collection

This calculation game, widespread throughout Africa, is sometimes called 'mankala' or 'solo'. The *wure* is a wooden structure made up of two lines of holes. Each partner has one line, which constitutes his 'camp', and a certain number of stones, or sometimes seeds or cowrie shells (Béart, p. 483; Popova, pp. 433-7). During his or her strategic moves, each player in turn takes a handful of stones, drops one per hole, and, in some versions of the game, attempts to leave the last one in the opponent's line (Deledicq & Deshayes, pp. 467-8). The success of imported European games, such as cards and draughts, has had the effect of this game falling out of favour in male circles, but some women, especially Wolof, have taken up this form of entertainment, despite the fact that it was originally invented for men (Popova, p. 439).

93
Gora Mbengue
Divination, 1982
33 x 48 cm (13 x 19 in)
Private collection

As noted earlier, many *marabouts* hold a plurality of functions: they are diviners, healers, magicians, men of prayer. This is ambiguous territory, where the old animistic practices combine with Islam in various ways. In this scene we see a woman perplexed. She sits in front of the *marabout* while he interprets the figures drawn by the cowries he has just thrown. The act of 'marabouting' someone consists of casting a spell on him or her by engaging a *marabout* as a sorcerer or magician: he is a sorcerer to the victim, but a magician to the person who commissions the intervention. Naturally, not every request to a *marabout* implies witchcraft. Indeed, the *marabout* is not necessarily an intermediary between two quarrellers, and he can simply intercede in favour of his client, for instance to assure someone that a forthcoming event of some importance will take place without any unfortunate incident marring it.

94
Gabou
The Shower, 1994
33 x 24 cm (13 x 9.5 in)
Private collection

Always the little voyeur dear to Gabou.

95

Mallos

Neurology, 1993

33 x 48 cm (13 x 19 in)

Royal Museum of Central Africa, Tervuren

This painting belongs to the series that Mallos dedicated to the subject of health and the various professions. It is treated as a comic strip, with the words and thoughts of the characters added.

96

Moussa Lo
Jamu, 1993
33 x 48 cm (13 x 19 in)
Private collection

Jamu is an operation that consists of having one's lips or gums tattooed. Wolof women (and women from other Senegalese ethnic groups) appreciate having black gums, which advantageously contrasts with the whiteness of the teeth. For this they use lemon-tree thorns or, more simply, in the cities, needles with which they prick their gums. The treated parts are smeared with soot or lamp-black that becomes encrusted in the wounded gums. The soot is generally what one can collect from the bottom of pots, while the lamp-black mostly derives from storm lanterns. Some women go through this painful treatment every year in order to revive the black, although the effect usually remains visible for four or five years.

97

Babacar Lo (Lô Ba)
The Tangana, no date
33 x 48 cm (13 x 19 in)
Royal Museum of Central Africa, Tervuren

The *tangana* is the simple breakfast that can be had for a reasonable price in the small, makeshift restaurants that are set up in the streets, most of which consist of a table and a couple of benches. *Tangana* consists of a piece of bread, buttered or not (according to one's financial means), and coffee (one spoonful of instant coffee, water, sugar and a lot of sweetened concentrated milk).

98
Jules
Two Women in Conversation, no date
(1993)
24 x 32 cm (9.5 x 12.5 in)
Royal Museum of Central Africa, Tervuren

99
Gabou
'Heavens, My Husband!', no date
33 x 48 cm (13 x 19 in)
Private collection

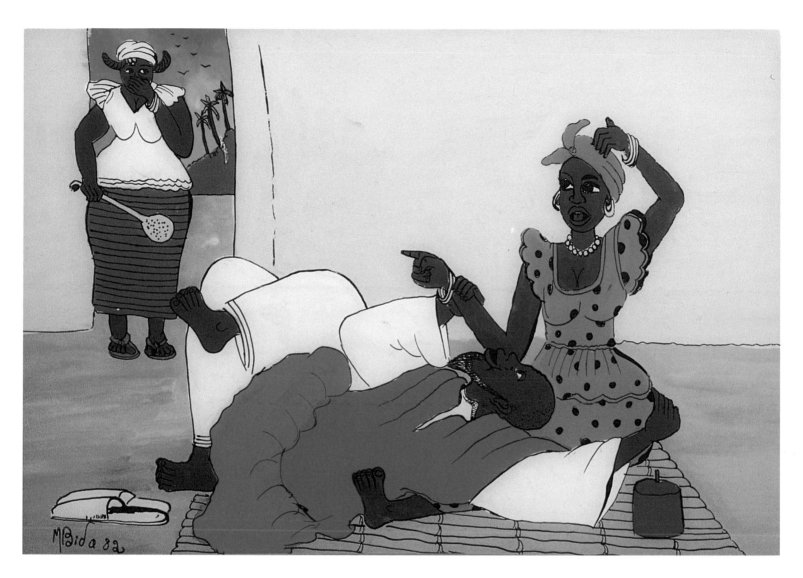

100
Mbida
'Heavens, Your Wife!',
1992
33 x 48 cm (13 x 19 in)
Private collection

After the cheated husband, the cheated
wife!

101

Azu Bade

'I'm going back to my mother's', 1993
33 x 48 cm (13 x 19 in)
Royal Museum of Central Africa, Tervuren

Here Azu Bade denounces forced weddings,
notably those involving young women offer-
ed by their families to some old *marabout*
whose protection they want to attract. What
happens in these cases is that the woman,
exasperated, leaves her unperforming
husband! This is a variation of a scene
frequently represented in reverse-glass
painting, where a woman is seen taking
her luggage and children and leaving a tearful husband behind her. Generally, repudia-
tions of this sort are made by the husbands,
but he is the chief victim here since he sees
the one who was at his service leave (see
Bouttiaux-Ndiaye, p. 29, fig. 22; Ndiaye,
K., p. 41-2).

102
Ibrahima Sall
The Stolen Child, no date
33 x 48 cm (13 x 19 in)
Private collection

103

Gora Mbengue

The Bay Fall and the Cockerel Thief,
1986

33 x 48 cm (13 x 19 in)
Royal Museum of Central Africa, Tervuren

The Bay Fall (see pl. 25) in the heat of
action in his role as a policeman.

104

Alexis Ngom

Two Thieves, 1993

33 x 48 cm (13 x 19 in)
Private collection

Two thieves are being chased. One of them
runs off as fast as his legs can carry him,
while the other has fallen and remains on
the ground, his toes spread stiff by fright.
Note how the impression of speed is rendered, with the legs of the still-running
thief stretched to 180 degrees. And, as
usual, there is an appropriate Wolof say-
ing: 'The hat never remains on the head of
him who is in trouble', for on the ground is
the discarded money-box with two large
coins in it.

105
Azu Bade
The Hen Thief, 1993
33 x 48 cm (13 x 19 in)
Royal Museum of Central Africa, Tervuren

Pursued from every quarter, this is a thief
who will not get away.

106

Khaly

The Thief and the Donkey, 1994

24 x 31 cm (9.5 x 12 in)
Private collection

This commissioned painting was intended for the 'Hé! bonjour Monsieur La Fontaine' exhibition (see note 56). It is an unusual piece since it illustrates a non-Senegalese theme, but it sits perfectly well in this category on tales and proverbs, all the more so since it has been touched up in the Senegalese fashion: the characters are African, as are the landscape and the clothes.

107
Mbida
The Story-teller, 1991
33 x 48 cm (13 x 19 in)
Private collection

108
Babacar Lo (Lô Ba)
The Baobab-Women, 1994
48 x 33 cm (19 x 13 in)
Royal Museum of Central Africa, Tervuren

A tale from Casamance: two young women are turned into baobab trees for mocking an elderly hunchback (Boisdur, p. 139). The moral of the story is a reminder of the strong respect in which the elderly are held in African societies.

109

Babacar Lo (Lô Ba)
Samba and the Guinarou, 1994
33 x 48 cm (13 x 19 in)
Royal Museum of Central Africa, Tervuren

An illustration of a famous tale concerning the adventures of a young prince in exile, Samba, who travels through the country accompanied by his servant, Dunguru, and his horse, Umullatomo. In the course of his travels, the prince is involved in frequent ex-ploits. At the end of the journey he reaches his goal and recovers his lost throne. This painting records an episode in Samba's adventures, his confrontation with Guinarou, a terrible monster. This dreadful creature – all scales, fangs and claws – haunts a lake to which it forbids all access. It spreads terror in the neighbouring village, whose inhabitants attempt to appease it by giving it a young virgin every year. Enters brave Samba. He first distinguishes himself by his temerity, for he refuses to retreat from the fire-spitting Guinarou. Impressed by his courage the monster offers him a weapon (a gun or spear, depending on the version), which will make him more powerful than other men. Samba accepts the gift and, on the pretext of trying out the quality of his spear, kills Guinarou. Having freed the village from terror and returned to the villagers access to the lake, Samba leaves to pursue his mission (Wisselman).

110

Alexis Ngom
Hunted Down, 1993
48 x 33 cm (19 x 13 in)
Private collection

An illustration of an aphorism concerning the inescapability and absurdity of human destiny. In trying to escape a lion, a man seeks refuge in a tree, unaware that a snake awaits him there. The hat that lies on the ground is a reminder that 'the hat never remains on the head of he who is in trouble'. Another Wolof proverb is also implicitly evoked: '*daw ba rëcc ci ngoore la bokk*', which means to run off as fast as one's legs can carry one is also an act of bravery (Ndiaye, K., p. 41).

111

Alexis Ngom

The Rescue of the Tamarind, 1993

48 x 33 cm (19 x 13 in)

Private collection

The theme is the same one as in plate 110, here rendered more complex by the presence of three participants trapped in a tamarind tree. Once again there is the lost hat.

Anonymous
The Torment of the Bad Wife, no date
36 x 47 cm (14 x 18.5 in)
Royal Museum of Central Africa, Tervuren

This painting illustrates a widely held belief, according to which a wife who does not behave well towards her husband during her life on earth will be punished after her death by the one she mistreated.

113

Alexis Ngom

The Torment of the Bad Master, 1993
33 x 48 cm (13 x 19 in)
Private collection

The assumption is the same as in plates 112 and 114, but this time it concerns the master who mistreated his animals.

114

Alexis Ngom

The Torment of the Bad Husband, 1993

33 x 48 cm (13 x 19 in)

Private collection

In this painting it is the husband who is punished for mistreating his wife during their time together on earth.

115
Alexis Ngom
The Restive Donkey, 1993
33 x 48 cm (13 x 19 in)
Private collection

The Wolof have a whole series of sayings
that insist it is futile to abuse an animal.
And, as we have seen (pl. 113), the price
to pay for bad deeds like the one shown
here can be very expensive, with endless
torment in the hereafter.

116

Babacar Lo (Lô Ba)
Farida the She-Donkey, 1994
33 x 48 cm (13 x 19 in)
Royal Museum of Central Africa, Tervuren

An illustration of a Wolof tale. Suffering from the drought, the donkeys do not know where they can find grass to feed themselves. Farida, the donkey, dreams up the stratagem of turning herself into a woman in order to seduce a man, then marry him, and thus gain access to his food. Then comes the end of the drought. Seeing the pastures verdant again, the donkeys visit Farida to present her with some fresh grass. On seeing her old companions once more, Farida is unable to contain herself and turns back into a donkey in front of an astonished husband. The moral of this tale is close to the expression 'What's bred in the bone will come out in the flesh'.

117
Gora Mbengue
Red Guard, 1981
48 x 33 cm (19 x 13 in)
Royal Museum of Central Africa, Tervuren

118
Babacar Lo (Lô Ba)
Mother with Child, no date
33 x 24 cm (13 x 9.5 in)
Private collection

119
Gora Mbengue
Tirailleur, 1983
48 x 33 cm (19 x 13 in)
Private collection

One of the heroic Senegalese infantrymen
who risked their own lives in someone
else's far-away cause (see note 45).

120
Moussa Lo
A Couple, no date
32 x 48 cm (12.5 x 19 in)
Private collection

121
Gora Mbengue
A Woman in Red, no date
48 x 33 cm (19 x 13 in)
Royal Museum of Central
Africa, Tervuren

122

Babacar Lo (B. Lô)
Woman with Libidor, no date
33 x 48 cm 13 x 19 in)
Royal Museum of Central Africa, Tervuren

Reproduced hundreds of times, this woman wearing her *libidor* is
one of the best-known images in reverse-glass painting. She is based on a photograph of Aba Segou, an elegant woman who was famous early this century. According to Babacar Lo, he made the first
painted image of her, after which all the traditional artists borrowed
it. This undated work goes back to the time when the eyes of Babacar Lo's characters were still set in an upward gaze, giving them a
somewhat melancholic air. He claims to have abandoned this manner because he noticed eventually that this phenomenon occurred
rarely and thus did not correspond to the reality he wanted to trans-
late. Aba Segou wears the *ngukke* hairstyle, which was popular in
her day, a headscarf (*musóoru bopp*) that matches her dress, and,
on her forehead, the famous *libidor*, a word that derives from the
French *louis d'or* (an old 20-franc gold piece).

123

Babacar Lo (Lô Ba)
Portrait of a Woman, 1993
65 x 48 cm (26 x 19 in)
Private collection

Shown in a kind of pose that is very unusual in traditional reverse-glass painting,
this woman squatting is another example
of Babacar Lo's great skill.

125

Mor Gueye

Two Women, 1993

33 x 48 cm (13 x 19 in)

Private collection

An interesting illustration of diverse jewelry, this painting shows two women in the traditional style of the frontal portrait that has its origins in photography. The woman on the left in green wears *bandal* or *libidor* on her forehead and what is called a *xob* (leaf) in her hair. The earrings (*jaaro nopp*) are *loŋ loŋ ak kaja*, *kaja* being the generic term for all jewels made in the shape of an acorn. Around her neck she wears a small necklace (*caq*) with a crescent moon, called a *dégu karaña*, then a *dégu kaja*, and finally a *caq u kaja*. The woman dressed in red also wears *libidor* on her forehead, as well as *karaña* at the tips of the two curved plaits of hair (an arrangement known as *gosi*; cf. Ashby Johnson, p. 46) and *kaja*. Her earrings are *loŋ loŋ ak ndumbël*, *ndumbël* being the term for the circular ball. Around her neck she wears a *dégu kaja* and a *sen u ndumbël* (*sen* is borrowed from *chaîne*, the French word for chain).

126
Alexis Ngom
The Serer Women, 1994
33 x 48 cm (13 x 19 in)
Royal Museum of Central Africa, Tervuren

This painting is a gallery of Serer hairstyles, though most of them can be found among the Wolof too. The ones shown here are, from left to right: *ndungu* in Serer and *nguke* in Wolof (see also pl. 122); *sek jid* (dry season and rainy season) in Serer (this hairstyle does not exist among the Wolof); *falaŋ* in Serer and *ben* in Wolof; *jañ* in Serer and *jamono kuro* in Wolof; another *falaŋ/ben*, and finally *cof togg* (all rises on top) in Serer and *faatu* in Wolof. The first and fifth women from the left are adorned with earrings called *sum sum* by the Wolof (these are the multiple rings fixed all round the ears), the third one is wearing Tukulor earrings called *dibé* (Ashby Johnson, p. 42), and, around the forehead, the woman on the far right is wearing what the Wolof call *tere-fal*. In addition, most of them wear *libidor* and *caq* necklaces similar to those shown in plate 125.

127
Mbida
A Couple, 1991
49 x 33 cm (19 x 13 in)
Private collection

The formal arrangement of these two
figures is strongly indebted to the art of the
photographic portrait. The side-table and
potted plant are features also to be found in
the repertory of photographic portraiture,
and in reverse-glass painting.

128
Metzo
Portrait of a Woman, 1993
33 x 12 cm (13 x 5 in)
Private collection

129
Metzo
Portrait of a Woman, 1993
17 x 16 cm (6.5 x 6 in)
Private collection

130
Metzo
A Fulbe Woman, 1993
33 x 24 cm (13 x 9.5 in)
Private collection

Immediately identifiable by the big golden
earrings and the amber balls held across
the top of the head, this woman is a classic
example of the Fulbe, famous for their
beauty.

131
Alexis Ngom
Polygamy, 1991
33 x 48 cm (13 x 19 in)
Private collection

The disproportionately large pipe signals to
us the husband's utter satisfaction with his
marital circumstances.

132
Mor Gueye
Polygamy, 1992
24 x 30 cm (9.5 x 12 in)
Private collection

A very stiff composition, reminiscent of
photographs, featuring a man with his
two wives.

133
Anonymous
Green 'diriyànke'
30 x 24 cm (12 x 9.5 in)
Private collection

A *diriyànke* is a woman of unusually attractive appearance. The green skin of the woman pictured here is a very special touch.

134
Babacar Lo (Lô Ba)
Mandionka and Kaleunkwe Ndiaye,
1993
33 x 48 cm (13 x 19 in)
Private collection

Babacar Lo is one of the most successful of those portrait painters who work on reverse-glass. For many commissions he works directly from photographs, though on occasion he paints actual subjects. The difficulty of working from photographs when a realistic portrayal of an individual is required arises from the need to paint an enlarged version of the photographed subject and, of course, to accomplish this in reverse. That is why the artist, when working on a portrait, is obliged frequently to turn over the glass to ascertain that the image imitates the photographed portrait as closely as possible.

135
Anonymous
Duck, no date
33 x 48 cm (13 x 19 in)
Private collection

136
Babacar Lo (Lô Ba)
Facing Cockerels, 1994
33×48 cm (13×19 in)
Royal Museum of Central Africa, Tervuren

137
Gora Mbengue
Calao and the Turtle, 1985
32 x 48 cm (12.5 x 19 in)
Private collection

138
Gora Mbengue (Mbeingue)
Calao, no date
48 x 33 cm (19 x 13 in)
Private collection

139

Gora Mbengue

Djiné, Ivory Coast, 1984

48 x 33 cm (19 x 13 in)

Private collection

Although there are Senegalese female water-spirits, this form of representing them is not a traditional one. The artist's title for this Gora painting is 'Djiné, Ivory Coast'. *Jinne* means spirit in Wolof. Images of this type are inspired by the Mammy Wata (from the English, Mammy Water) found in the Gulf of Benin, more specifically in the Nigerian region of the Cross River. They have very long hair and hold snakes in their hands (Bol, pp. 24-5), an image that has its origins in a German chromolithograph (see fig. 11, p. 20) showing an Indian snake-charmer (Salmons, pp. 8-15). The Mammy Wata of the Gulf of Benin should not be confused with those of Zaire, who have a fish-tail like the mermaids we find in Western art.

140
Gora Mbengue (M'beingue)
Djiné, Ivory Coast, no date
48 x 33 cm (19 x 13 in)
Private collection

141
Magatte Ndiaye
Mammy Wata, no date
48 x 35 cm (19 x 14 in)
Private collection

A Mammy Wata with fish-tail, an unusual
composition in West African art.

142
Magatte Ndiaye
The Target, 1994
48 x 35 cm (19 x 14 in)
Royal Museum of Central Africa, Tervuren

This recent painting by Magatte Ndiaye is
a good example of his unusual repertory.
According to the artist, at the time he was
working on The Target he was undergoing
treatment with drugs, and his hand was
therefore less assured than formerly.

143

Amadou Diop

'L'oreille cassée', 1993

32 x 24 cm (12.5 x 9.5 in)

Private collection

A beautiful example of a reproduction from a comic-strip, in this case a Tintin album cover, 'The Broken Ear'.

144

Anonymous
In the Desert, no date
42 x 48 cm (16.5 x 19 in)
Royal Museum of Central Africa, Tervuren

This scene, perhaps inspired by the Tunisian tale of Antar and Abla (Renaudeau & Strobel, p. 55), is a complete departure from the landscape of Senegal, for here the setting is one of the great deserts to the north.

145
Gora Mbengue
Christ on the Cross, 1982
48 x 32 cm (19 x 12.5 in)
Private collection

A rare example of Christian subject-matter
in a reverse-glass painting.

146
Paco
Desert and Dromedaries, no date
23 x 48 cm (9 x 19 in)
Private collection

147
Amadou Sow
Untitled, 1993
65 x 50 cm (26 x 20 in)
Private collection

148
Hassane Sar
Untitled, 1993
Private collection

149
Serigne Ndiaye
L'Aristo, 1993
35 x 25 cm (14 x 10 in)
Private collection

150
Sea Diallo
Nemali I, 1988
35 x 35 cm (14 x 14 in)
Private collection

A Senegalese woman replete with mysterious, captivating charm. Here she is
shown shaking her *boubou* above a vessel
containing burning incense *(cuuraay)*. Both
men and women often infuse their clothes
with perfume in this manner.

Bibliography

Ashby Johnson, M.   1994
   'Gold Jewelry of the Wolof and the Tukulor of Senegal', *African Arts*, XXVII/1, pp. 36-49, 94-5.
Aziza, Mohamed   1978
   L'image et l'islam. L'image dans la société arabe contemporaine. Paris: Albin Michel.
Barbin, C.   1984
   'A Senegalese Painter puts his Memories under Glass', *Unesco Features*, no. 75.
Béart, C.   1955
   Jeux et jouets de l'Ouest africain, II: Dakar: IFAN. (Mémoires de l'Institut français d'Afrique noire, no. 42).
Boisdur, M.H.   1981-82
   Contacts de civilisations au Sénégal. Le phénomène de la peinture sur verre, PhD thesis, Paris: Université de Paris I.
Bol, V.   1994
   'Une peinture dite populaire', in *Papier blanc, encre noire. Approches des peintures d'Afrique centrale*, ed. M. Quaghebeur, Bruxelles: Communauté française de Belgique (Cellule Fin de siècle).
Bourlard, I.   1987
   'L'icône peinte sous verre de la Vierge au manteau des Musées royaux d'Art et d'Histoire', *Bulletin des Musées Royaux d'Art et d'Histoire*, pp. 131-60.
Bouttiaux-Ndiaye, A.-M.   1993
   'Peintures sous verre du Sénégal', *Africa Museum*, I, pp. 8-39.
Brincard, M.-Th. & Dedieu, M.   1986
   Treasures of a Popular Art: Paintings on Glass from Senegal. New York: African-American Institute.
Cruise O'Brien D.B.   1971
   The Mourides of Senegal: The Political and Economic Organization of an Islamic Brotherhood. Oxford: Clarendon Press.
Cruise O'Brien D.B.   1979
   'Confréries musulmanes en Afrique noire', in *Contribution (La) du christianisme et de l'islam à la formation d'Etats indépendants en Afrique au Sud du Sahara. Textes et documents du colloque sur l'Afrique, Bonn-Bad Godesberg, 2-4 May 1979.* Stuttgart: Institut für Auslandsbeziehungen.
Dancu, J. & Dancu, D.   1979
   Die bäuerliche Hinterglasmalerei in Rumänien. Bucharest: Meridiane Verlag.

Dedieu, M.   1986
   'Une Afrique peinte sous verre: l'imagerie colorée des "souwères" sénégalais', in *Senegal Narrative Paintings.* Lafayette (Louisiana), New York: University Art Museum, African American Institute.
Deledicq, A. & Deshayes, P.   1976
   'Exploitation didactique du "wari"', *Cahiers d'Etudes africaines*, XVI/3-4, pp. 467-97.
Diop, Abdoulaye-Bara   1981
   La société wolof. Tradition et changement. Les systèmes d'inégalité et de domination. Paris: Karthala.
Diop, Aram & Calvet, M. & Dia, Oumar Ben Khatab   1971
   Les cent et les quinze cents mots les plus fréquents de la langue wolof. Dakar: Centre de linguistique appliquée de Dakar (Les langues africaines au Sénégal, 41).
Diouf, Mamadou   1992
   'Islam: peinture sous verre et idéologie populaire', in *Art pictural zaïrois*, ed. B. Jewsiewicki. Québec: Editions du Septentrion.
Drioton E. & Vandier, J.   1975 (1938)
   L'Egypte. Des origines à la conquête d'Alexandrie. Paris: Presses universitaires de France.
Encyclopaedia of Islam   1927
   A Dictionary of the Geography, Ethnography and Biography of the Muhammadan Peoples, ed. M.Th. Houtsma, A.J. Wensinck, T.W. Arnold, W. Heffening and E. Lévi-Provençal. Leyden: E.J. Brill; London: Luzac & Co.
Erman, A.   1952
   La religion des Egyptiens. Paris: Payot.
Fal, Arame & Santos, R. & Doneux, J.L.   1990
   Dictionnaire wolof-français suivi d'un index français-wolof. Paris: Karthala.
'Fixé (Le) sous-verre: interview Mor Gueye'   1989
   Le Baobab, Oct-Nov, no. 4.
Gaudefroy-Demombynes, M.   1969
   Mahomet. Paris: Albin Michel (L'évolution de l'humanité).
Gaudibert, P.   1987
   'Introduction historique', in 'Souweres. Peintures populaires du Sénégal', *Cahiers de l'ADEIAO*, 4.

Gaudibert, P.   1991
   L'art africain contemporain. Paris: Editions Cercle d'Art (Diagonales).
Gaye, El-Hadji Mouhamadou Sakhir & Sylla, Assane   1972
   '"La vie de Seydina Mouhamadou Limâmou Laye" par Cheikh Mahtar Lo', *Bulletin de l'IFAN*, series B, XXXIV/3, 497 523.
Gouilly, A.   1952
   L'islam dans l'Afrique occidentale française. Paris: Editions Larose.
Harden, D.B.   1987
   Glass of the Caesars. Milan: Olivetti.
Johnson, G.W.   1979
   'William Ponty and Republican Paternalism in French West Africa (1866-1915)', in *African Proconsuls: European Governors in Africa*, ed. L.H. Gann and P. Duignan, New York, London, Stanford: Free Press, Hoover Institution.
Le Cour Grandmaison, C.   1972
   Femmes dakaroises. Rôles traditionnels féminins et urbanisation. Abidjan: Université d'Abidjan. (Annales de l'Université, series F, 4).
Lexique wolof-français   1976
   Dakar: Centre de Linguistique appliquée de Dakar.
Marone, Ibrahima   1970
   'Le tidjanisme au Sénégal', *Bulletin de l'IFAN*, series B, XXXII/1, pp. 136-215.
Monteil, V.   1964
   L'islam noir. Paris: Seuil.
Monteil, V.   1966 (a)
   Esquisses sénégalaises (Wâlo-Kayor-Dyolof-Mourides-Un visionnaire). Dakar: IFAN (Initiations et Etudes africaines, XXI).
Monteil, V.   1966 (b)
   'Le Dyolof et Al-Bouri Ndiaye', *Bulletin de l'IFAN*, series B, XXVIII/3-4, pp. 595-636.
Monteil, V.   1969
   'Marabouts', in *Islam in Africa*, ed. J. Kritzeck & W.H. Lewis, New York, Toronto, London, Melbourne: Van Nostrand-Reinhold Company.
Moreau, R.L.   1982
   Africains musulmans. Paris, Abidjan: Présence africaine, Inadès Edition.
National Archives of Senegal. File 19 G. 4. 1906-1917
   Propagande islamique par l'image et la presse.

Ndiaye, Fr.   1977
'La création plastique, artisanale et architecturale', in *Patrimoine culturel et création contemporaine en Afrique et dans le monde arabe*, ed. Mohamed Aziza. Dakar, Abidjan: Les Nouvelles Editions Africaines.

Ndiaye, Kelountang   1993
'Contes, proverbes et dictons dans la peinture sous verre du Sénégal, in 'Peintures sous verre du Sénégal', *Africa Museum*, I, pp. 40-43.

Ndiaye, Serigne   1989
'Die Hinterglasmalerei', in F. Axt, and El Hadji Moussa Babacar Sy, *Bildende Kunst der Gegenwart in Senegal*, pp. 165-68.

Ndiaye Leyti, Oumar   1966
'Le Djoloff et ses bourbas', *Bulletin de l'IFAN*, series B, XXVIII/3-4, pp. 966-1008.

Painter, K.   1987
'Groups J and K: Introduction', in *Glass of the Caesars*. Milan: Olivetti.

Piress, J.   1992
'Le fixé selon Serigne Ndiaye', *Le Soleil*, 11 June.

Popova, Assia   1976
'Les mankala africains', *Cahiers d'Etudes africaines*, XVI/3-4, pp. 433-58.

Renaudeau, M. & Strobel, M.   1984
Peinture sous verre du Sénégal. Paris: Fernand Nathan; Dakar: Les Nouvelles Editions Africaines.

Salmons, J.   1977
'Mammy Wata', *African Arts*, X/3, pp. 8-15, 87-8.

Samb, Amar   1969
'Touba et son "Magal"', *Bulletin de l'IFAN*, series B, XXXI/3, pp. 733-53.

Samb, Amar   1971
'L'islam et l'histoire du Sénégal', *Bulletin de l'IFAN*, series B, XXXIII/3, pp. 461-507.

Samb, Amar   1972
Essai sur la contribution du Sénégal à la littérature d'expression arabe. Dakar: IFAN.

Searing, J.F.   1993
West African Slavery and Atlantic Commerce. The Senegal River Valley, 1700-1860. Cambridge: Cambridge University Press (African Studies Series, 77).

Shaw, Th. M.   1986
'Sacred and Profane Aspects of the Popular Image of Sheikh Amadou Bamba', in *Treasures of a Popular Art: Paintings on Glass from Senegal*. New York: African-American Institute.

Silla, Ousmane   1966
'Persistance des castes dans la société wolof contemporaine', *Bulletin de l'IFAN*, series B, XXVIII/3-4, pp. 731-70.

Silla, Ousmane   1968
'Structure familiale et mentalité religieuses des Lebou du Sénégal', *Notes africaines*, no. 119, pp. 79 83.

'Souweres. Peintures populaires du Sénégal'   1987
Cahiers de l'ADEIAO, 4.

Strobel, M.   1982
L'imagerie religieuse au Sénégal, PhD thesis. Strasbourg: Institute of Ethnology.

Ströter-Bender, J.   1991
Zeitgenössische Kunst der "Dritten Welt". Äthiopien, Australien (Aboriginals), Indien, Indonesien, Jamaica, Kenia, Senegal und Tanzania. Cologne: Dumont Buchverlag.

Ströter-Bender, J.   1993
'Hinterglasmalerei in Senegal' in *Afrika – Iwalewa, Kunstforum*, vol. 122, pp. 188-9.

Sy, Cheikh Tidiane   1970
'Ahmadou Bamba et l'islamisation des Wolof', *Bulletin de l'IFAN*, series B, XXXII/2, pp. 412-33.

Sylla, Assane   1971
'Les persécutions de Seydina Mouhamadou Limamou Laye par les autorités coloniales', *Bulletin de l'IFAN*, series B, XXXIII/3, pp. 590-641.

Sylla, Assane   1978
La philosophie morale des Wolof. Dakar: Sankoré.

Thomas, L.V.   1958-59
Les Diola. Essai d'une analyse fonctionnelle sur une population de Basse-Casamance. Dakar: IFAN (Mémoires de l'Institut français d'Afrique noire, 55).

Vogel, S.   1991
'Urban art: Art of the Here and Now', in *Africa explores*, ed. S. Vogel. New York: Center for African Art; Munich: Prestel.

Wisselman, N. & de Renty, Y.   1975
Samba et le Guinarou. Une partie de la légende héroïque de Samba Guéladio Diegui. Dakar, Abidjan: Les Nouvelles Editions Africaines.

Photographic Acknowledgements

All photographs were taken by Jean Marc Vandyck (Royal Museum of Central Africa, Tervuren), except for the following:

figs. 1, 12 and all photographs of the artists (except that of Gora Mbengue): A.-M. Bouttiaux-Ndiaye, Brussels
fig. 8: ACL, Brussels

plates 12, 42, 43, 81 and the photograph of Gora Mbengue: M. Renaudeau, Paris
plate 100: P. Cassard, Paris
plate 147: St. Gueye, Dakar
plate 148: Bouna Medoune Seye, Dakar
plate 149: Toure Mandemory, Dakar
plate 150: Sea Diallo, Dakar